MUSIC AND ITS STORY

MUSIC AND ITS STORY

by

Robert T. White

YESTERDAY'S CLASSICS

ITHACA, NEW YORK

This edition, first published in 2022 by Yesterday's Classics, an imprint of Yesterday's Classics, LLC, is an unabridged republication of the text originally published by Cambridge University Press in 1924. For the complete listing of the books that are published by Yesterday's Classics, please visit www.yesterdaysclassics.com. Yesterday's Classics is the publishing arm of Gateway to the Classics which presents the complete text of hundreds of classic books for children at www.gatewaytotheclassics.com.

ISBN: 978-1-63334-164-7

Yesterday's Classics, LLC
PO Box 339
Ithaca, NY 14851

PREFACE

THIS BOOK should be regarded rather as an introduction to the study of Musical History than as a history in itself. There seems to be a demand for a small manual dealing in a simple way with the growth and development of Music as an art. The advanced student will find all the information he needs in many excellent modern text-books, and the connoisseur is also well provided for. But almost all of these books are too detailed and statistical for the average student, and still more so for that large and growing section of the public which desires to be conversant with musical matters, but is not prepared to wade through volumes that deal with musical works which are never likely to be heard again.

I have endeavoured to treat the subject concisely, as well as from a broad standpoint; hence the reader must expect to find that the names of many worthy musicians whose work was of more interest to their contemporaries than to posterity are omitted. Mere biographical details are but sparingly introduced; my chief aim has been to deal with music rather than with musicians, most of whom were very ordinary mortals in mundane affairs. Within the limits prescribed, it has been impossible to discuss at all fully the developments which have taken place during the last fifty years; I have therefore preferred to indicate the general trend of modern music.

No apology is needed for the insertion of a list of gramophone records, chosen not so much from a recreative as from a historical point of view. Even so, such a list must be very incomplete, since the process of recording is being rapidly improved, and manufacturers of records are becoming more and more enterprising, especially in the reproduction of long instrumental works without "cuts." It is hardly conceivable that anyone will attempt in future to teach musical history without availing himself to the full of the great assistance afforded by the gramophone, player-piano and "wireless."

Hearty thanks are due to Professor Raymont, M.A. and to Mr Forbes Milne, M.A., Mus.Bac. for the kind assistance they have given in the preparation of this book. Also I desire to thank Messrs Hawkes and Son, of Piccadilly Circus, for their kind permission to include illustrations from their catalogue of Wind Instruments.

R. T. W.

UNIVERSITY OF LONDON,
GOLDSMITHS COLLEGE.

October, 1924.

CONTENTS

CHAPTER I

THE BEGINNINGS OF MUSIC

IN ordinary speech we often use words to which everyone attaches a definite meaning; and yet if we are asked to state exactly what their meaning is, we find it difficult to frame a satisfactory answer. Such terms, for instance, as "beauty," "truth," "colour," "electricity," are hard to define, yet they have a real meaning for everybody who uses them. The use of the term "Music" is common enough, but nobody has yet found a satisfactory reply to the question "What *is* Music?" At any rate, such definitions as have been given are not very intelligible to ordinary folk. But it is quite possible to say a good deal about the material out of which Music—as the term is commonly used—is made.

Musical Material. This material is *Sound,* but out of the multitude of sounds which can be made, only a very few are used for musical purposes. Sound is the result of vibration: if one strikes a low note on the pianoforte, the string can be seen in a state of violent agitation. Also if a drum be struck, and the fingers placed lightly on the parchment, the vibrations can easily be felt. These vibrations give rise to corresponding vibrations in the surrounding air; thus air-waves are produced, just as

1

water-waves are formed when a stone is thrown into a pond, and æther-waves are produced by an electric discharge, as in "wireless." These air-waves spread outwards in all directions, and when they reach the ear they give rise to a sensation known as *sound*. The human ear is not sensitive enough to appreciate all sounds. If the vibrations are fewer than about twenty per second, or more rapid than about thirty-eight thousand per second, the ear in most cases does not respond. It is interesting to note that some animals, especially dogs, can detect sounds which are too high in pitch for us to distinguish.

Scientific instruments have been invented which make it possible to *see* the vibrations of sounding bodies. In the case of a certain class of sounds it is seen that the vibrations are perfectly regular; whilst in other cases the vibrations are irregular. This difference may be shown thus:

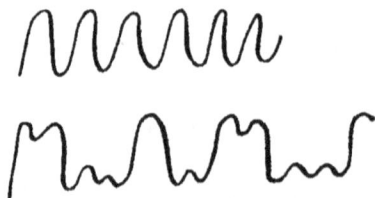

The sounds produced by regular vibrations are called by the scientist "musical" sounds; the others he terms "noises." The ordinary person, however, has to rely on his ear, not on his eye, to decide whether a sound shall be called a "musical note" or a "noise"; he generally regards a musical note as a pleasant sound; a noise as an unpleasant sound. Even so, much difference of opinion notes, while others were mastered by notes." Josquin, in his best moments, realised that music which pleases the ear is more valuable than that which merely astonishes by its cleverness; but even so, there are in his music long passages which are too crude for us to enjoy.

There was still only one sphere of musical work in which a serious musician could hope to make a living; that was in composing music for the Church and securing a good rendering of it. Most princely courts of that time maintained a private chapel and a well-trained choir under the direction of a competent musician. There was much competition between the courts as to which could secure the services of the best composer and choir-master. Also the various Town Councils were proud of their church choirs and more especially of their organs and organists; while in great cathedrals such as St Peter's at Rome and St Mark's at Venice no pains were spared in providing the best music which could be obtained. The principal service of the Catholic Church is High Mass; hence the chief occupation of musicians was writing and rehearsing settings of the Mass, although there are many other portions of the Liturgy which demand a musical setting. The "Motet,"[19] corresponding to the English Church "Anthem" of to-day, was always an important musical item.

Contrapuntal Ingenuity. The tendency already mentioned for composers to write music which would impress other musicians with its cleverness was noticeable all through the fifteenth century. The

[19] Records Nos. 3 and 4.

usual plan followed in writing a Mass was to take one or more phrases from a well-known Plain-chant tune and interweave other original tunes with them, introducing such devices as Canon. If the harmony which results is complete and satisfactory, and the sentiment of the words is mirrored in the music, well and good. But this process is a difficult one, and too often the Netherlanders were engaged in "going one better" than their colleagues in making difficulties for themselves, and then showing how these might be conquered. Now, unfortunately, the average listener (the musical layman) knows nothing of the difficulties of Counterpoint and Canon. A composer, by taking infinite pains, may be able to write a piece of music which will sound the same whether it is played forwards or backwards, although it is almost impossible to do this so that there will be no disagreeable clashing between the parts. But even supposing that such a piece of music has been written, the listener will not be able to recognise the topsy-turvy feature of the tune, so that if the piece does not *sound* well the composer's pains have been wasted. This point has to be emphasised because it crops up not only in the fifteenth but also in the succeeding centuries. Many modern composers overlook the fact that only a very few listeners can detect musical cleverness: it is the general effect—the *sound*—which appeals to them. However, when we come to consider the music of the sixteenth century we shall find that some composers successfully grappled with the problem, and made it possible for a composer like Bach or Wagner to write music, which, besides being ingenious enough to interest people who can detect cleverness when it is present, is also expressive and agreeable to listen to. Few of the many thousands of people who have been thrilled by the first chorus of Bach's *Matthew Passion* realise that the composer set himself a task involving the exercise of unlimited cleverness in combining two choirs and two orchestras with the addition of another small choir.

Rise of Secular Music. In another direction great changes were taking place. Hitherto the professional musicians had confined their attention almost entirely to sacred music, but about this time secular music began to take a position of importance. As we have already seen, Folk-song—the music of amateurs—flourished quite independently of Church-music. Here there was nobody to say "You *must* sing thus," or "You *must* write your music in accordance with this or that set of rules." The ballad-singers and wandering minstrels were to be met with in every country. Often they were a nuisance, as they got to know too much of what went on in the rival courts. The melodies sung by the people, as well as those invented by the ballad-singers and minstrels (who, in a sense, were professionals), were not complicated by the addition of harmony and counterpoint. Included amongst the early Folk-songs we often find popular carols and hymns for which no place was provided in the Catholic liturgy; these were invented by the people themselves and were merely tolerated by the church authorities. Guilds and societies were formed whose object was to encourage the singing of ballads and simple songs. The Crusaders were accustomed to enliven their long marches with the singing of popular hymns and songs. Singing, too, was a regular feature of pilgrimages. As early as 1221 St. Francis writes: "There is a certain country called 'Germany,' wherein dwell Christians who come into our land; they visit all the thresholds of the holy shrines, and sing hymns of praise to God and His saints."

Music Guilds. Not only the common people, but princes and knights joined these Guilds. One, the "Minnesingers," was very active in Germany—we still possess more than fifteen hundred of their songs. This Guild held public competitions, something like the Welsh Eisteddfodau of to-day. The Minnesingers attained the summit of their influence in the early part of the thirteenth century. In France we find the Troubadours and Trouvères who cultivated literature, poetry and prose, as well as song. King Richard I was a Trouvère. In the fourteenth and fifteenth centuries the "Mastersingers" were very influential. They, also, held competitions governed by very strict rules, and no one was allowed to become a member of the Guild who could not pass a stiff examination in the composition of songs. The famous opera by Richard Wagner entitled *Die Meistersinger* is really an elaborate skit, but also something more than a skit, on the practices of the Mastersingers. The most celebrated Mastersinger was a cobbler, Hans Sachs (*b.* 1494), who settled in the great "Free City" of Nuremberg. Five large volumes of his songs were published in 1558.

The melodies written and sung by members of these Guilds were of a very simple kind. Most of them were attached to poems dealing with love and chivalry, and many of the tunes were annexed by Luther and his colleagues of the Reformation when they compiled the *New Order of Service* for use in the Reformed Churches. Brief mention must also be made of the Mystery and Miracle plays so popular in the Middle Ages. Familiar hymns and carols were generally introduced into these performances; the great musical Forms known as Opera and Oratorio can be traced back to Mystery and Miracle plays.

Influence of the Guilds. Although the enormous literature of mediaeval songs and ballads was accumulated with scarcely any help from professional musicians, it was inevitable that sooner or later they would have to take it into account. The principal effect of the popularity of this Guild-music upon "Art-music" was to make composers lay more stress upon the importance of melody. We have already seen that the "Art-music" of this period was strictly contrapuntal, at any rate for lengthy works. This implies generally, that no one voice is more prominent than any other. Also, if it should happen that the composer allotted a continuous melody to one voice, usually the tenor, this was frequently obscured by the other melodies. [In this connection one may think of "general conversation" in a drawing-room.] The general complaint against contrapuntal music by those who have not had a good musical education is that "there is no tune in it." What is really meant is that they cannot follow a tune which is interwoven with other tunes more or less of the same nature. Now the earliest composers of secular music, e.g. the Mastersingers, concerned themselves but little with Counterpoint, and not much with Harmony; for them, the tune was the thing. Contact with Guild-music led the composers of "Art-music" to pay attention to the desirability of writing tunes easily grasped, and not hidden by the presence of several subordinate tunes. (Cf. our modern hymn-tune in which the treble part is all-important; the other voices are added merely to produce harmony.)

It must, however, be noticed that while contrapuntal music became more "tuneful," the general principles of Counterpoint were still adhered to for all serious works of any length.

In England, music made little advance during the fifteenth century. Music requires for its cultivation a reasonably prosperous and peaceful state of society, and this condition did not hold in England at that time. The Wars of the Roses plunged the country into misery which was not assuaged until the strong hand of the Tudor sovereigns made short work of sedition.

On the whole, the music of the fifteenth century is more interesting to the historian than agreeable to the listener of to-day—indeed, in its original form, it could hardly be included in a modern programme. But there is quite another tale to be told about the music of the next century.

CHAPTER VIII

MUSIC IN THE SIXTEENTH CENTURY

FROM the musical point of view, the sixteenth century is remarkable for six reasons:

1. Purely devotional music reaches its highest point of excellence.

2. With the Reformation a somewhat new type of sacred choral music attains prominence.

3. Secular vocal music of real worth competes with sacred music.

4. Instrumental music, as an independent Art-Form, begins to assume the high position it has since held.

5. In England, under the Tudors, both sacred and secular music is written which is at least as valuable as that produced on the continent.

6. The invention of music-printing from music-type makes it possible for composers of different nationalities to get into touch with each other's work.

Pure Choral Music. By about the middle of this century composers of music for use in church had formed a definite idea as to the style of music best suited for that purpose. It is not easy to explain this style to those who have not heard examples of it, but, fortunately, it is becoming more and more common for competent church choirs to include sixteenth century music in their repertoire; and, as will presently be seen, gramophone records will give a fair notion of the chief features of this unique type of music. But any attempt to reproduce it on the pianoforte gives one quite a false notion of its peculiarities. In view of the renewed interest taken in this music an attempt must be made to describe it. The lines upon which composers worked were somewhat as follows:

1. The music should be written for a choir, unaccompanied.

2. It should be devotional in character, and regarded rather as an aid to devotion than as the chief feature of the service.

3. It should be strictly "modal," and founded upon the old Plain-chant.

4. In the main, it should be contrapuntal; the resulting harmony should be smooth, consisting only of common chords and their inversions, ornamented by passing and auxiliary notes.

5. No strong contrasts of any kind ought to be introduced unless demanded by the sentiment of the words; and, in any case, the contrasts were not to be violent.

The views of the ecclesiastical authorities on these points are well expressed in the *Motu Proprio*[20] of Pope Pius X on Sacred Music. Paragraph 12 runs: "Except the chant of the celebrant and the sacred ministers of the altar, which must always be sung in Plain-chant without any accompaniment, the rest of the liturgical singing belongs properly to the choir of clerics: wherefore singers in church, if they are laymen, are the substitutes of the ecclesiastical choir."

Let us consider in order each of the five points noted above. The Catholic Church has always claimed that "the proper music of the Church is only vocal; although the accompaniment of an organ is permitted at times, bands are strictly forbidden to play in church." Hence composers of the sixteenth century were forced to think in terms of unaccompanied vocal music alone when writing for the Church.

Secondly, it must be remembered that during the greater part of the time that music is sung at Mass, certain ceremonial acts of great importance are proceeding. Moreover, the faithful are encouraged to proceed with their private devotions whenever, so far as the congregation is concerned, there is a pause in the progress of the Mass. Consequently, merely pretty or sensational music would call too much attention to itself and disturb the religious atmosphere.

Mode and Key. The third point is not so easy to explain. It has already been said in Chapter v that every Plain-chant melody is written in one or other of the

[20] Catholic Truth Society. Price 1*d.*

65

twelve Modes, and very seldom does any melody depart from the strict rules governing that mode. (Modern music, on the contrary, depends for its effect largely on changes of mode and key.) Moreover, each Mode has its own appropriate harmonies. This adherence to one Mode all through a composition gives rise at first to a feeling of monotony in the case of the listener to-day, but this feeling soon wears off in the pleasure of detecting interesting details of which this type of music is full. Another reason why modal music sounds quaint to us is that composers of this period had not yet acquired that strong sense of "key" which we possess. It would not be advisable to explain here the exact difference between "key" and "mode," but it may be pointed out that "accidentals," as we call them, were freely employed in the sixteenth century, not with any idea of change of key, but merely to get variety by turning a minor into a major chord, or to make a phrase easy to sing. To us, such a phrase as G, F sharp, G occurring in a piece in C major would give the feeling of a modulation into key G, and we should probably expect this phrase to be harmonised as at *(a)*, but a sixteenth century composer would be just as likely to harmonise it as at *(b)*.

Tallis' Litany as sung in English churches to-day furnishes an excellent example of the variety which can be obtained by substituting major for minor chords, and shows, incidentally, how much less strong was the sense of "key" in those days. Cf.:—

W. Parsons

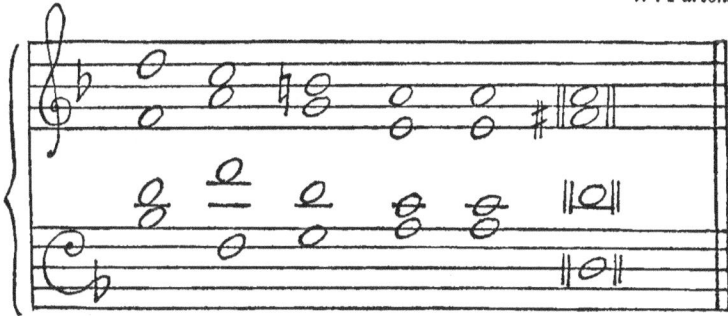

Thomas Tallys

And take not Thy Ho - ly Spirit from us.

Contrapuntal Devices. Fourthly, the contrapuntal principle was fully accepted as being the most suitable for general adoption. It is very rare indeed to find anything like a modern hymn-tune, with its melody in the treble part, and plain harmony below. By far the greater number of the Church compositions open thus: a short phrase, perhaps taken from a Plain-chant melody, is sung by one set of voices, this is taken up by each of the other voices in turn ("Imitation"), meanwhile new melodic fragments are interwoven with the original.

Then another little phrase will be introduced and tossed about between the voices. When the imitation is strict and continuous we have a Canon. The similarity of the above to a "Round" will be noticed.

To appreciate fully this type of music demands much closer attention than can reasonably be asked for from most listeners. One must be able to follow the progress of two, three, or more tunes sung together, and this ability is possessed only by a very few. However, there is an intense pleasure to be gained merely from listening to the web of sounds and the musical conversation carried on between the different voices.

Vittoria

The fifth point has a close connection with the second. Modern music is full of violent contrasts; of volume of tone, speed, key, rhythm, harmony, and so forth. But startling contrasts, especially those produced by unexpected harmonies and remote changes of key, would certainly interfere with devotional exercises; therefore the best music of this period is never violently exciting. There is plenty of variety of a subtle kind, but unless the words demand a distinct change of character in the music (e.g. "He suffered and was buried"; "the third day He rose again") one can be sure that the composer will go on in much the same way as he began. By comparing the beautiful "Amen" by Vittoria quoted on p. 68 with the extract given on p. 50 it will easily be seen that a considerable advance in expressiveness had been made during the sixteenth century.

Palestrina. The names which stand out must strongly amongst the large number of Church composers of this period are Orlando di Lasso (Netherlander), Vittoria (Spaniard), and Palestrina (Italian). The English composers will be considered later. The greatest of all was Palestrina (*d.* 1594). During the course of his long life he was fully employed in providing settings of the Mass[21] and other parts of the Catholic Liturgy and was so successful that he is universally accepted as the greatest composer who had as yet appeared. Sooner or later it was certain that some composer would arise who would demonstrate that it would be impossible to proceed further on the same narrow lines. That composer was Palestrina; no one, before or since, has written finer music in this particular style, and with his death a chapter of musical history came to a close. In considering the Catholic Church music of the sixteenth century it must not be overlooked that we are dealing not with crude works which to-day make no appeal,

[21] Record No. 1, also H.M.V. D 336.

but with real live music which is performed constantly by choirs which are able to grapple with the serious difficulties so often met with in the music of Palestrina and his contemporaries.

CHAPTER IX

MUSIC AND THE REFORMATION

WHILE Catholic Church music was progressing on the lines indicated in the previous chapter, the principles of the Reformation were spreading rapidly. It is not necessary here to go into the questions of doctrine which divided Catholics and Evangelicals, but only to trace the effect of the Reformation upon the art of Music. The great Reformer, Luther, was himself a cultured musician, with an intense regard for the music of the Catholic Church. He was very anxious that Church music should not suffer by reason of any alterations in the conduct of Divine Service which were necessarily brought about by the acceptance of the new doctrines. But in one direction a very important development took place.

Congregational singing. Hitherto, as we have already seen, the rendering of musical portions of the Catholic Liturgy had been confined to the choir and clerics, although the Church did not discourage what may be termed "Religious Folk-Hymns" which had no place in the Liturgy itself. It occurred to Luther and his friends that it would be well to make use of the fact that the German people were exceedingly fond of singing and that they already possessed a large store of tunes which, with only slight alterations, would be suitable for use in church. Also, one of the changes which were introduced into the *New Order of Service* was the substitution of German for Latin in certain parts of the Liturgy. Hence an opportunity arose of introducing congregational singing. All that was necessary was to secure some sacred poems in German which could be sung to simple tunes. A beginning was made by taking some of the Canticles, the Creed, the Lord's Prayer, etc., and putting them into a metrical form so that they became, as it were, congregational hymns. Obviously the next step was to write sacred poems which were not merely paraphrases of the Canticles. The first Lutheran hymn-book, containing only a few hymns, was published in 1524. This proved very popular, and soon a large number of hymn-books appeared. The production of "Chorals" was so rapid that by the end of the eighteenth century poets of varying degrees of culture had written at least 73,000 hymns.

The Choral. Whence came the tunes to which these hymns were sung? At first they were drawn from two sources. The more simple Plain-chant tunes already well known were annexed, and some of the more difficult of such tunes were used in a simplified form. Considerable use was also made of Folk-song melodies; the staid German Folk-tunes were particularly suitable for conversion into hymn-tunes. The melodies of some of the best-known Chorals were originally composed for secular words; e.g. the famous "Passion Choral" tune beginning

is the melody of a love-song[22].

As the number of hymns increased, more tunes had to be provided. The great composers of the time, with very few exceptions, left this task to men who, while not clever musicians, yet had a happy knack of inventing tunes easy to sing and devotional in character. Clearly, little else is required in a congregational hymn-tune, so that one would expect to find that the hymn-tune, as a musical Form, would not suffer much change. However, as will presently be seen, quite elaborate compositions could be written using the Choral as a basis.

Although but little can be written here about the history of hymn-tunes, one must not belittle their importance. For a very large number of people hymn-singing constituted by far the greater part of their musical activities. Hymn-singing does not demand much musical ability; opportunities of exercising this ability are frequent, and it certainly corresponds to the universal desire to connect music with religion. If one of the chief functions of music be to influence the feelings or emotions, then the value of hymn-singing is obvious. One need hardly refer to the overwhelming

---

[22] An interesting example of a country-dance tune converted into a hymn-tune is the melody usually sung to the Palm-Sunday hymn, "All glory, laud, and honour." This is only a version of "Sellenger's Round."

effect of a familiar hymn sung by a large gathering at some solemn religious function.

Metrical Psalters. The Reformers were not exactly a happy family; the history of the relations between the Calvinists who had their headquarters at Geneva and the followers of Luther proves this only too well. This is reflected also in the difference of character between the Lutheran and Calvinist hymn-books. The latter party consisted mostly of French-speaking converts; consequently the German Choral did not strongly appeal to them. Instead, they developed a form of hymnody which had been occasionally practised for many years past. This consisted of metrical versions of the Psalms of David; i.e. the Psalms were put into simple ballad-metres so that they could be sung as hymns. At first only a few selected psalms were treated in this fashion; additions were made until in 1562 a complete metrical Psalter in French appeared with the title *Les Pseaumes mis en rime françoise par Clément Marot et Theodore de Beze.* No fewer than twenty-four editions of this work appeared in the same year; in it were incorporated one hundred and twenty-five melodies. Even the French Catholics used this book. Later, it became the official hymn-book of the Huguenots. There was considerable intercourse between the Huguenots and the Reformers in England and Scotland during this period; also the latter were in touch with the developments taking place in Lutheran Germany. Although some few attempts had been made quite early in Britain to versify parts of the Psalter, it was not until the Reformation gained a firm footing in England that psalm-singing after the

Calvinistic fashion became popular. It was the metrical Psalter of Geneva rather than the devotional Choral of Germany which appealed most strongly to the British people. Indeed, for many a long year, Psalm-singing from a metrical version, not hymn-singing in the ordinary sense, was the universal practice in England and Scotland.

English Psalters. A goodly number of French and German tunes became popular in our country; the "Old Hundredth" is one of these. It would be beside our purpose to describe all the metrical Psalters which appeared in England; it need only be said that a version of the Psalter by Sternhold and Hopkins (the *Old Version*) published in a complete form in 1562 became the more or less official hymn-book of the Protestant Church in England. This was afterwards superseded by the *New Version* by Tate and Brady, first published in 1696. From a literary point of view both of these versions were very crude—especially the *Old Version,* e.g. Psalm cxxxvii:

> When as we sate in Babilon,
> The ryvers round about,
> And in remembrance of Sion
> The teares for grief burst out;
> We hanged our harpes and instruments,
> The willow trees upon,
> For in that place men for their use
> Had planted many a one.

A fair number of the metrical psalms from the *New Version* are still to be met with in modern hymn-books; e.g. "All people that on earth do dwell" (Psalm c), "As pants the hart," "Through all the changing scenes of life."

The usual practice was to write the real tune in the tenor part, and to add bass, treble, and alto parts above or below; this meant, of course, that *all* members of the congregation, unless they could read music easily, sang the tenor part, the other parts being given to the choir and organ. An old term "Faux Bourdon" was applied to this procedure; in many churches of to-day this custom is being revived. A good specimen of Faux Bourdon is familiar to most church-goers in the *Festal Responses* by Thomas Tallys: the real tune of nearly all of these is in the tenor part. (This is exemplified in the "Response" given on p. 67.)

Whilst the *New Order of Service* encouraged the congregation to take, musically speaking, a more active part in worship, this did not mean that hymn-singing supplanted entirely the older contrapuntal style of music which was reaching such a pitch of excellence

in Catholic circles. Luther was very keen on retaining this wherever possible. However, Lutheran composers began to give up the old Plain-chant tunes as a basis for their long compositions: they chose familiar chorals instead. The above example is by Heinrich Isaak, perhaps the most prolific German composer of the sixteenth century. Observe that the chief melody is in the highest part, not in the tenor.

CHAPTER X

SECULAR MUSIC

IN the sixteenth century the Church was no longer almost the only patron of the arts; wealthy laymen— princes, merchants, and municipal authorities—offered a career to artists who hitherto had been obliged to confine their attention to the requirements of the Church. A certain amount of secular music had been written in the fifteenth century, notably by Dufay, but mostly as a kind of "side-line." In the sixteenth century attempts were made to provide choirs with secular music as a relief to the Masses, Motets, and other sacred works, the rendering of which occupied most of their energies.

Madrigals. The earliest secular music of any real importance took the form of Madrigals. These were compositions of a reasonable length, set to secular words and written for three or more voices without instrumental accompaniment. Composers were at first shy of making these works very different in style from the contrapuntal Masses and Motets. Indeed, the only apparent difference between a Madrigal and a Motet was that the words of the former were secular and the music was presumably sung at a greater speed. But as the early Madrigals found much favour, composers tried to evolve a style which would not seem to be a mere copy of the prevalent type of sacred music. In fact they realised that the sprightly songs of the people contained features well worth introducing into Madrigals. Consequently it is found that in a goodly number of the sixteenth century Madrigals the rhythms are more simple and regular, the melodic phrases are more tuneful, the counterpoint is less complicated so that much more frequently all the parts would be singing the same word at the same moment, and a cheerful mood is more in evidence. The writing of Madrigals came to be regarded as a no less honourable occupation than the composition of Masses. A very large number were written by Roman and Venetian composers especially; nearly all of these can be listened to to-day with much pleasure, provided that they are well sung. The English Madrigalians will be referred to later. It should be reiterated that all Madrigals are for a choir unaccompanied; playing them on a pianoforte gives only a distorted idea of their excellences.

The Organ. Perhaps even more important than the rise of the Madrigal was the growing interest in instrumental music. Clearly there can be no good instrumental music unless there are satisfactory instruments available for its rendering. So far, the only instrument which had reached a fair standard of excellence was the organ; naturally so, because its proper place is in a church, and church music had been fostered more consistently than secular. Every church of any importance in this century had an organ upon which much money and skill had been expended. Even so early as 1516, for instance, the church of St. Mary at Lübeck possessed a large organ with two manuals and pedals. That being the case, one would expect to find that organ music had attained some degree of excellence, but, unfortunately, organists were too prone to "show off" by writing music which consisted of little else than series of rapid scale- or arpeggio-passages interspersed with heavy lumps of chords. In fact it was much like bad improvisation. It was not until late in the century that composers began to solve a problem which confronts every composer of instrumental music, viz. what are the good and bad points of any instrument, and what is the type of music which will best bring out the former and hide the latter.

Clavichord and Harpsichord. Two other keyboard instruments were in common use at this time, viz. the clavichord and the harpsichord. (The spinet and virginal were small varieties of the latter instrument.) As a great deal of fine music was written for both instruments, it is well to try to understand their peculiarities. Open the pianoforte, take out the "action," and with the back of a pen-knife strike one of the longer strings (say, D on the middle line of the bass stave) and *keep the knife pressed on the string* after it is struck. Two different notes will be faintly heard. Repeat the operation at another point on the same string; again two notes will be heard, but these will not be the same as before. Notice that the sound is very faint and that it dies away immediately. This experiment explains the principle of the clavichord. Now *twang* (not press) the string with the blade of the knife in two or three places; notice that you cannot now obtain notes of *different* pitch from the one string; also that it is possible to produce a fairly loud sound, and that the sound does not die away so quickly. This illustrates the principle of the harpsichord. It is unnecessary to give a picture of the harpsichord, since in outward appearance a large harpsichord is very much like a "grand" pianoforte. In the case of the clavichord the striking was effected by a small piece of brass (the tangent) which flew upwards when the key was depressed; a piece of felt prevented the shorter segment of the string from sounding. The twanging of the string in the harpsichord was effected by a small piece of quill or hard leather which was projected upwards when the key was depressed. In spite of the fact that only a very weak tone can be obtained from the clavichord, it remained for long a popular household instrument; Bach preferred it to the harpsichord, and his famous *Forty-eight Preludes and Fugues* were written for the clavichord. The organ, harpsichord (with its smaller counterparts, the virginal and spinet), and clavichord were the only keyboard instruments in common use until the invention of the pianoforte in the eighteenth century.

Of what nature was the first music written for clavichord and harpsichord? As a matter of fact, composers hardly knew what to do. The instruments clearly had their limitations. Since neither could sustain a sound for more than a fraction of a second or so, it was of little use to write music of the type most suitable for voices. Moreover, on both instruments the range of tone-volume was small; if one played *pianissimo* on the clavichord

Spinet

the sound could hardly be heard, and *fortissimo* on the harpsichord was painful. If a hymn-tune was played slowly there would be annoying silences between the chords. These could certainly be filled up by all kinds of "ornamental" notes and other devices, and this makeshift was commonly employed. But both instruments had one virtue: the sound produced was very clear, so that contrapuntal passages could be easily followed and the separate melodies readily distinguished. Hence the best music written for these instruments was contrapuntal in character, the Fugue being a very popular form[23].

[23] Harpsichord music is represented by Records Nos. 8, 9, 10, 11; also H.M.V. E 294 and 295.

Couperin

The Viol. Stringed instruments played with a bow had been in existence since very early times, even outside Europe; but these instruments were clumsy and the tone obtainable was far from pleasant. In the sixteenth century the principal representative of this family of instruments was the Viol. In shape much like the stringed instruments used to-day, it was less graceful in appearance; the back being flat instead of rounded, while the bow was altogether more clumsy.

Viols of different sizes were made, corresponding to Treble, Alto, Tenor and Bass. Perhaps the most popular viol was the "viol da gamba," the forerunner of the modern 'cello. A "chest," *i.e.* a complete set of viols, was to be found in most wealthy households. The only real viol in use to-day is that called the "double bass," which occupies such an important place in the modern orchestra. It is not known who actually invented the violin—the modern equivalent of the treble viol—but in the latter part of the sixteenth century we find Andrea Amati and Gaspard di Salo making violins, violas and violoncellos of such excellence that, although inferior to the splendid instruments made in the next century, they were much nearer perfection than any other instrument of the period. Nevertheless, it took some time for composers to discover how best to utilise bowed instruments. At first they seem to have been used only in conjunction with the voice; although pieces were written and described as "apt for viols or voices." This meant that the Soprano part, instead of being sung, could be played on the Treble viol, the Alto part on the Alto viol, and so forth. No doubt the players also had a little musical frolic occasionally on their own account, but composers were slow in recognising that the style of music most suitable for stringed instruments was not that which was best suited to the voice.

The Lute. The other favourite instrument at this time was the Lute. Instruments of this type had been used for centuries. In shape, the lute is something like a mandoline, but the belly is proportionately larger, and the strings are plucked by the fingers instead of being twanged with a plectrum. As in the case of the viols, lutes were constructed in varied sizes; the bass lute ("Theorbo") was a very ornate instrument of considerable dimensions. The use of the lute seems to have been mostly confined to the accompaniment of vocal music; not a great deal of music was written especially for the lute, although this instrument occupied a prominent place in the orchestra of that period. As a solo instrument, the lute had all the disadvantages of

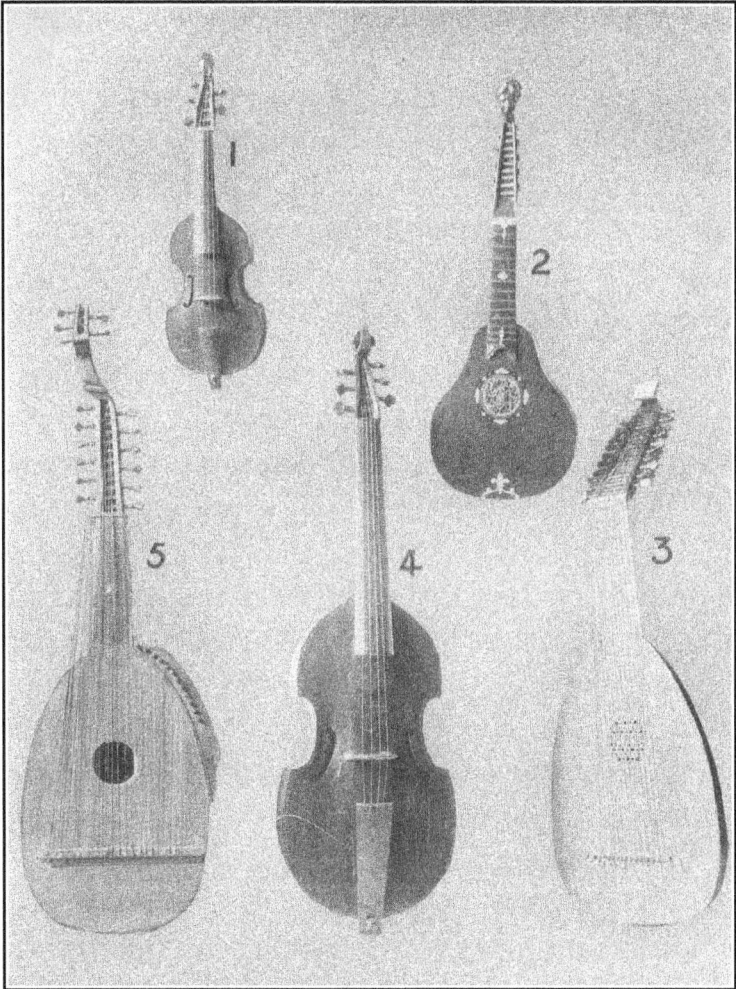

1. Viol.   2. Cithern.   3. Lute.   4. Viol da gamba.
5. Lute with additional harp-strings.

EARLY INSTRUMENTS

the harpsichord, and some peculiar to itself. In the first place, a good lute was expensive to make and expensive to keep in order; it was not an instrument for the poor man. However careful the maker was in choosing well-seasoned wood, a slight variation of temperature caused the wood to "buckle," and this meant that it was very difficult to keep the instrument in tune; strings also were continually breaking. It was said that a lute-player spent more than half his life in keeping his instrument in order.

Every princely court had its band. This was always in evidence at ceremonial functions and royal entertainments[24]. Henry VII's band comprised fourteen trumpets, three lutes, three rebecs (primitive fiddles), three tambourins and four tambours (both a species of drum), one harp, two viols, one cornmeuse (a kind of bagpipe) and ten trombones. When all were playing together the noise must have been fearsome. Other instruments incorporated in the royal bands of the period were recorders (a species of flute, or rather flageolet), and wooden instruments with a cup-shaped mouthpiece such as the cornet (not identical with the modern brass instrument of that name), shawm and bombard, the two latter being the forerunners of our oboe and bassoon respectively. With such a heterogeneous collection of instruments the serious composer could not do much; but the band was well constituted to "make a joyful noise," and no more was expected from it.

[24] See Chap. IX in Stanford and Forsyth's *History of Music.*

We have said already that there was hardly any branch of music which was not well represented in England under the Tudor sovereigns, and it will be interesting at this stage to consider the subject in more detail.

CHAPTER XI

TUDOR MUSIC

THE close of the Wars of the Roses found England in a bad way. Most of her ablest sons had shed their blood on the battlefield, and it seemed as if recovery would be a very slow process. However, Henry VII was an exceedingly strong and determined ruler, and under him the fortunes of the country were in a great measure re-established. Conditions were favourable to progress in music and literature, and fortunately the King took a great deal of interest in music. As mentioned in Chapter X, he maintained an extensive musical establishment at court, and the choir of the Chapels Royal was a very live body of musicians. The new process of music-printing made it possible for English musicians to become familiar with the music of the Continent, and it was soon proved that our composers could hold their own with the best of the Flemish and Italian writers.

Unluckily, music-publishing in England had hardly yet begun to thrive; and though the musical output in Tudor England was enormous, only a small percentage was published. Manuscript copies, however, were multiplied and a great number eventually found their way into cathedral and collegiate libraries, and into private collections. It is only comparatively recently that any attempt was made to unearth this mine of wealth, and the result has proved surprising. It had not been suspected that Tudor music was not only of great interest to the antiquarian, but was as beautiful in itself as the best work of the Flemings and Italians. This music, moreover, was not the product of only one or two men of genius; there were quite a goodly number of English composers who were capable of writing music of the highest quality, music which affords considerable pleasure to a twentieth-century audience. The early Tudor composers—of whom Fairfax and Taverner were the chief—followed continental practice in writing Masses, Motets and Madrigals of the familiar type.

Musical Activity in England. But it was in the reigns of Henry VIII, Mary and Elizabeth that English music reached a standard of such excellence that it has never been surpassed in its own particular line. It is true that it was mainly in the sphere of unaccompanied choral music that English composers shone, but this is the case with all composers of that time. Now the music was written not merely to be looked at, but performed; and we know that performances were frequent. Considering the great difficulty of much of this music, together with the fact just mentioned, it is clear that the standard of musical education must have been high. For a long time music had occupied a prominent place in education. The principal aim of educational institutions seems to have been to train boys so that they could take their part in the services of the Church—so that Latin and Music were the subjects which received most attention. In fact "Song-schools" were attached to most cathedrals and large monasteries. But Madrigals and Ballets were sung not only by professionals but by amateurs; it was considered that a man was badly educated if he could not take part in a Madrigal. Some have argued that, since a good deal of this music is very difficult to sing, therefore only a few gifted amateurs could have sung it. This does not follow. Music had become almost a fashionable craze, and in order to conform to a fashion people will take considerable pains. Besides, the reading of music is not difficult provided that one begins early and is prepared to spend much time in becoming expert. The school curriculum was not overcrowded with subjects in those days, and there were fewer distractions.

Amateur composers were numerous. King Henry VIII was no mean musician. One of his songs is on the opposite page.

The Reformation. It is interesting to observe the effect of the Reformation upon Tudor music. Some composers, like William Byrd, who was probably the greatest composer of this period, held fast to the old religion; others, like Marbecke, embraced the doctrines of the Reformed Church. Others, again, like Thomas Tallys, were more pliable, and agreed with whatever party happened to have the upper hand. The truth is that the Tudor sovereigns did not want to lose the services of a good musician, provided that he was prudent enough not to advertise his religious opinions. More than once Elizabeth had to interfere to prevent

TUDOR MUSIC

THE KYNGE'S BALADE   *King Henry VIII*

Past - ime with   good   com - - pan - y   I
Grudge who will, but   none   de - ny,   So

1st.   *2nd*

love, and shall un - til   I die.
God   be pleased, this   life   will I.   For

my past-ance, hunt, sing and dance, my   heart   is   set,   All

good - ly sport   to   my com - fort, Who shall   me   let?

one of her favourite court musicians from getting into trouble with the authorities. This accounts for the fact that some musicians like Tallys wrote not only for the Catholic but also for the Protestant Church.

We have seen that Psalm-singing was introduced into England and Scotland in Tudor times. Also it is worthy of note that Marbecke adapted the old Plain-chant to many sections of the First Prayer-Book of Edward VI, and that Tallys wrote his well-known *Preces*, *Responses* and *Litany* for the Second Prayer-Book.

Madrigals. But the particular musical form in which

91

the English writers of this period shone conspicuously was the Madrigal. According to Forsyth, nearly two thousand Elizabethan madrigals are now in print, most of them being perfect specimens of the form. Especially interesting and effective are the "Ballet-madrigals." "Now is the month of Maying" and "Since first I saw your face" are typical specimens: these are very much like the modern part-song, in so far as the interest is mainly melodic and harmonic rather than contrapuntal. The melody is almost always in the treble part throughout, so that the Ballet-madrigal could fairly well be sung as a solo-song with lute or viol accompaniment. The rhythm was usually not complicated, so that the whole composition was quite easy to sing. Notice that here we have, almost for the first time, a distinctive form of secular vocal music which is not a mere copy of the sacred contrapuntal music of the period, but which is much more akin to Folk-music. The greatest monument to the skill of the English Madrigalian composers is the magnificent collection called *The Triumphs of Oriana,* written by representative composers in honour of Queen Elizabeth ("Oriana")[25]. The principal Madrigal composers of the period were Byrd, Dowland, Morley, Wilbye, Weelkes and Orlando Gibbons[26].

Virginal Music. It should be remarked that at this time public concerts were unknown; indeed it was not until the latter part of the seventeenth century that they became a regular feature of musical life in England.

[25] These are published in separate numbers by Messrs. Novello, also by Messrs. Stainer and Bell.

[26] See Records Nos. 5, 6, 7.

Apart from Church music and that performed in the open air or at court functions, there was nothing but what the Germans call *Haus-Musik*—music performed in private or at social gatherings. Pompous and strident music would have been out of place under such conditions, but the Madrigal, Ballet, and the music of slight texture written for harpsichord, clavichord or lute was exactly suitable. It is necessary to make a few remarks on the harpsichord music of this period. The limitations of this instrument have already been described, and although the Tudor composers did not regard instrumental music as being on such a high plane as the Madrigal, they wrote a good deal of music for this instrument as well as for viols and lutes. Some of it has been preserved in the two collections known as *Lady Nevell's Booke,* in which all the pieces are by William Byrd, and the *Fitzwilliam Virginal Book.* Most of the pieces are very slight. The latter book was not compiled until the reign of James I, but the tunes in it were popular in Tudor times. Many of them are Country-dance tunes with Variations; others are original tunes of the dance type; others, again, are song-tunes[27]. A large number of these tunes have been edited and published lately. "Old English Suite" by Bantock, published by Messrs. Novello, contains some representative pieces.

In Elizabethan times the "folk" were also musically active. Well-known ballads dating from this period are "The Bailiff's Daughter of Islington," "Greensleeves," "The British Grenadiers," "The Carman's whistle," and "A poor soul sat sighing."

[27] Record No. 11. See also *Harpsichord Music* by John Bull and Orlando Gibbons, published by Joseph Williams.

" Jhon come kisse me now."

William Byrd. Amidst the many musicians of the Tudor period who may be styled "great" in the particular fields of musical composition in which they worked William Byrd stands conspicuous. He was born *c.* 1542, became organist of Lincoln Cathedral, and, in 1569, a Gentleman of the Chapels Royal. Together with his godfather, Thomas Tallys, he obtained from Elizabeth the monopoly for printing and selling music and music-paper, and very soon he began to issue Motets in the approved contrapuntal style. In 1588— the year of the Armada—he published *Psalms, Sonets, and songs of Sadnes and Pietie.* In a quaint Preface he tries to "perswade eueryone to learne to sing," for, among other reasons, "It doth strengthen all parts of the brest, and doth open the pipes." Also—and this is significant of the attitude of serious composers of the period towards instrumental music—"There is not any Musicke of Instruments whatsoeuer comparable to that which is made of the voyces of Men where the voyces are good, and the same well-sorted and ordered." In the writing of Madrigals, both serious and light, he became an acknowledged expert and his Virginal music was much played. His settings of the Mass, now frequently performed, are very fine. He was regarded by his English contemporaries as the greatest musician of the time, and, although a Catholic, his powerful friends seem to have protected him from persecution. In 1597 he retired to a country estate in Essex, where he busied himself in composition until his death at the age of 81.

It is only within recent years that Byrd's music has again become widely known. Although in most of his choral works he used the musical phraseology of the period, his music for stringed instruments foreshadows the great achievements of later classical composers, and even those of us who have to make his acquaintance chiefly through the medium of some excellent gramophone records[28] must realise the attractiveness and worth of his compositions.

Although after the death of Byrd there was considerable musical activity in England, and a good deal of interest was evinced in the new developments taking place in Italy, France and Germany, yet English music no longer maintained the high position reached under the Tudors. The Puritans, though not antagonistic to the claims of music in general, did their utmost to discourage elaborate Church music. One name, however, stands out prominently during the Restoration period—that of Henry Purcell, to whom reference will be made later.

---

[28] In addition to the records named in the Appendix, readers are especially advised to obtain E 291 (H.M.V.).

CHAPTER XII

OPERA AND ORATORIO

IN 1602, Caccini, an Italian, published *Le Nuove Musiche*. What was "new" about this music? It was a small collection of pieces—in very free rhythm—for a single voice, with an accompaniment consisting of a succession of chords to be played on a harpsichord or big lute. To us this idea does not seem anything of a novelty, but observe how it differed from the type of music hitherto in favour amongst serious musicians: the "New Music" was not choral, nor was it purely instrumental, neither was it in any sense contrapuntal. The volume in question gives the fruit of many experiments made between about 1594 and 1602. At this time Florence was probably the wealthiest city in Europe, and her chief citizens took a pride in supporting liberally all artistic enterprises. One of the most enthusiastic patrons of music was Count Bardi, who was especially interested in the attempted revival of Greek plays, or rather in the application of the best features of these plays to the dramatic performances which had become so popular in Florence. Now, while it was quite possible to get a good idea of the general scope and "lay-out" of the Greek dramas (because the text of many had been preserved), yet, for reasons already explained, no practical knowledge of the music could be obtained.

The "Nuove Musiche." Bardi therefore called into consultation the most eminent Florentine composers, and between them they invented the *Nuove Musiche*. After several experiments had proved that this type of music would serve the purpose, Peri, in 1600, composed an "Opera" founded on the old Greek story of "Euridice." This was lavishly staged and was greeted with enthusiasm. The important musical form called "Opera" was thus firmly established, and most ambitious composers turned their energies in this direction. Notice that this involved a radical departure from the principles of Counterpoint which had for so long governed musical composition. We now have not so much an interweaving of several melodies, but rather *one* melody supported by chords. Harmony takes precedence over Counterpoint, and instead of being as it were the *result* of the combination of melodies, it takes an independent place in the musical scheme. The chords favoured by the older composers were of the simplest character, viz. "common chords" and their inversions; discords, when used at all, were set in such a context that they were hardly felt as discords at all. But the prominence now given to harmony tempted composers to experiment with discords on a more extensive scale. The boldest experimenter was Claudio Monteverde; he introduced discords and progressions of chords which must have thrilled—pleasantly or unpleasantly—his contemporaries; even to-day the

results of some of his experiments astonish us by their
novelty, not to say ugliness. Cf.

Recitative and Aria. It would hardly be profitable
to give a list of the earliest Operas; they are never
performed nowadays, as all their best features have been
adopted and improved upon by later composers. In all
of them the various forms of "Recitative" occupied the
most prominent place. The type of Recitative already
referred to is called "Recitativo secco," and was largely
employed by composers for nearly two hundred years.
It may be regarded as the "prose" of music. Obviously,
some variety was needed, and the next step was the
utilisation of the orchestra, instead of one or two instruments only, for the purposes of accompaniment. This
necessitated more or less "strict time" and allowed of
the chords being broken up into little rhythmic figures
which gave life and interest to the whole. A further
step was taken when the "Aria" (supposed to have been
invented by Alessandro Scarlatti, *d.* 1725) came into
vogue. It may roughly be described as a somewhat
lengthy song—often very elaborate—accompanied by
an orchestra. Handel's *Messiah,* although an oratorio
belonging to the eighteenth century, illustrates very well
the conventional types of Recitative. No. 15 is a good

example of "Recitativo secco," No. 16 is a specimen of the Recitative in strict time with orchestral accompaniment, and No. 6 illustrates the Aria form. Short choruses were introduced into Opera quite early, and the principal soloists sometimes joined forces in rendering duets, trios, quartets, etc. Short interludes for the orchestra were provided, and the rapid improvements made in orchestral instruments during the eighteenth century gave composers an incentive to bring the orchestra into greater prominence, although the Italian composers have always favoured the singers more than the instrumentalists.

Spread of Opera. The cult of Opera rapidly spread in other countries. In France, Louis XIV gave much encouragement to French composers, who evolved an operatic style of their own. This made much more use of ballet-dances, which had always been popular in France. Clearly this meant that the band had to be more seriously considered. The most prominent figure in French musical circles was Lulli, the "Maître de Musique" to Louis XIV. With him, the Overture, which before his time was merely a string of meagre phrases of no real significance, became a real orchestral piece comprising generally two or three contrasted movements. The first was usually a slow and stately piece, the second a lively movement involving the combination of melodies (a reversion to Counterpoint) and sometimes a Minuet or other dignified dance-tune was added. (See the Overtures to Handel's *Messiah* and *Samson.*)

In Germany also Opera won great favour. The chief centre was Hamburg. At first only Italian Operas were presented, but soon German composers, notably Richard Keiser, set to work on their own account. Handel produced here his first four operas. By the end of the seventeenth century composers had become so expert in writing operas that a very few weeks sufficed for most of them to produce a new work. The plots were too often of the flimsiest character and were merely pegs on which to hang Recitatives and Arias. The soloists were masters or mistresses of the situation, and all that the composer was expected to do was to provide them with showy solos. A good deal was demanded from the stage-manager; sumptuous scenery was thought a necessity, but good acting was a subordinate requisite. To-day this inequality is not tolerated by a critical audience, and these seventeenth century operas are mostly regarded as of historical interest only. However, there are signs of the revival of interest in the best of these early operas, and some, especially those by Handel, receive an occasional performance. "Italian Opera," using the term in its technical sense, although overshadowed in recent times by the "Music Drama" as exemplified in Wagner's works, still appeals to a large number of lovers of Opera.

Oratorio. Oratorio came into being almost exactly at the same time as Opera. Also, at first, there was little difference between them, except that the Oratorio was founded upon a religious subject, whereas Opera was based on a secular story. There was nothing new in the idea of the dramatisation of a sacred story with the addition of music; the old Miracle and Mystery plays are instances to the contrary. But in these music occupied a secondary place. At the time when the "New Music" was beginning to create a stir, sacred dramas with music were looked upon with favour by some influential ecclesiastics—notably by S. Philip Neri—who were rather afraid that the new Operas would injure the cause of morality and religion. The new style of sacred drama as performed in the "Oratory" attached to Neri's church came to be known as "Oratorio." The first Oratorio performed in public was on the subject of the Soul and Body, and in style was similar to the first Opera; both appeared in 1600. Thereafter, for a long time, Oratorio and Opera proceeded upon parallel lines; the main difference, other than that between the subjects chosen for musical treatment, was that the Chorus in Oratorio was of more importance than in Opera. As the reader is never likely to hear any of the earliest Oratorios, it is not necessary to discuss them further.

Passion Music. While Opera and Oratorio almost monopolised the attention of musicians in France and Italy during the seventeenth century, great advances in other directions were being made in Germany. We have seen that quite a large amount of musical literature had grown up round the Protestant Choral; also many passages from the Bible, especially from the Psalms, had been set to stately music, notably by Heinrich Schütz. At the same time composers for the organ began to be agreed on the type of music best fitted for this instrument and the orchestra had been introduced into the church, although not as yet taking a very prominent part. The most interesting development of sacred music in connection with the Lutheran Church is concerned with the elaboration of "Passion Music" and the "Church Cantata." Very early in the history of Christianity it was the custom during Holy Week to recite the narrative of the Passion in a dramatic form by allotting the words of Christ to one reader, those of the Evangelist (the Narrator) to another, those of Peter, Pilate, and other minor characters to a third, and the ejaculations of the disciples and the mob to a fourth.[29] Later, those who under took these roles sang their phrases to a simple Plain-chant formula, while the words of the crowd were sung by the choir in simple harmony. This method of singing the *Passion* is still adhered to in the Roman ritual. The only opportunity afforded to a composer in this connection is clearly the elaboration of the choruses. Even so, since the ceremonial singing of the *Passion* is a lengthy task, the choruses had to be very concise. Many composers wrote dignified settings of these short choruses; those mostly used to-day were written by Vittoria and Soriano. In 1573 the first German *Passion* was produced, and the development of Passion Music as a distinct musical form hereafter was wholly confined to Lutheran composers. Briefly, the changes which took place were as follows. First of all, Chorals to be sung by the congregation were introduced at suitable places, and instrumental support for the voices was provided. Next, the old Plain-chant melodies sung by the Narrator

---

[29] In several of the Passion settings the individuality of the personages is frequently not reflected in the music; e.g. the words of Christ are sometimes allotted to a four-part Chorus. The Matthew Passion is sung every year at St Paul's Cathedral on Tuesday in Holy Week.

and other single personages were discarded; for these melodies was substituted original "Recitative." The instrumental part now had to become more prominent. It only remained to introduce some Arias, for Passion Music to approximate to Oratorio. This development took place at the beginning of the eighteenth century, when certain minor poets in North Germany wrote poems on the *Passion* expressly intended to be set to music. In the most popular of these is introduced a mythical character, the "Daughter of Sion," who comments or reflects upon the incidents of the story. These comments, put into versified form, furnished composers with texts for Arias and choruses. It was

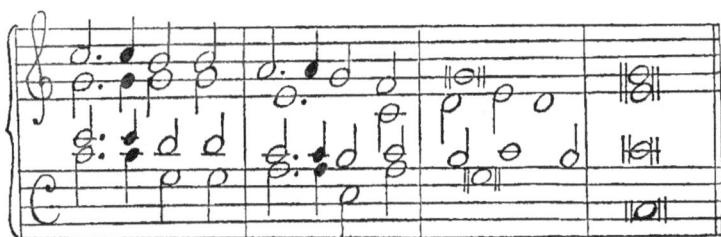

Cru-ci-fi-ge, Cru-ci-fi-ge e · · · um.

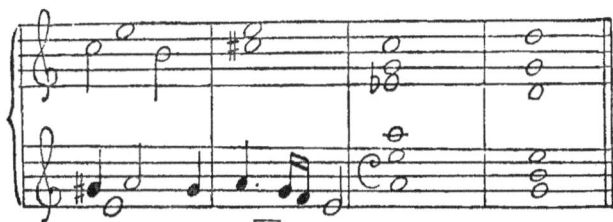

Creut - ze Je - sum.

Let Him be cru - · · · ci-fied

Let Him be cru - -

&c

upon this model that Bach wrote his great *Passions*. These will be referred to later. As time went on, Passion Music as far as the Germans were concerned differed in no vital particulars from Oratorio. It may be interesting to compare three settings of the same words from the Passion. The suave, devotional style of the first example by Asola (1595) is in strong contrast with the daring modulation in the next by Demantius (1631), while the sinister, rasping effect of the setting from Bach's *Matthew Passion,* heightened as it is by the orchestral accompaniment, could only have been obtained by a composer with a keen sense for the dramatic.

The Church Cantata. We have seen that one result of the "New Music" was to make instrumental accompaniment more of a necessity. As soon, therefore, as this new style of music was introduced into the Lutheran Church we find the orchestra admitted also. It became common to introduce into the service a long composition for voices and orchestra which to-day is called a "Church Cantata." It is practically a long Anthem with orchestral accompaniment. It takes very many forms; perhaps the following is as common as any: (1) a Chorus, with independent accompaniment founded on a Choral; (2) a Recitative, leading to one or more Arias for soloists; (3) the original Choral in simple form. Very often for the opening Choral is substituted an elaborate fugal chorus; and not infrequently no Choral is introduced—the Cantata then becomes nothing but a short Oratorio. It was J. S. Bach who later on brought the Church Cantata to perfection; his *Christmas Oratorio* is really a collection of six Cantatas. After his death the Church Cantata merged into Oratorio. In England the place of the Church Cantata was taken by the "Full Anthem," which in plan differed little from the Cantata except that the Choral was not employed, although orchestral accompaniments were frequently provided.

The Masque. Although, as we have said, the rate of musical progress in England during the Stuart period had somewhat slackened, yet there was a considerable development of an old form of entertainment called the "Masque." In its earliest stages this was an outdoor pageant in which music was very prominent. The acting—such as it was—was undertaken by amateurs, the rendering of the music being left to professionals. A pageant performed at Richmond Palace in 1512 is thus described:

> The King, with eleven others were disguised after the manner of Italy called a Mask, a thing not seen before in England. They were apparelled in garments long and broad, wrought all with gold, with visors and caps of gold; and, after the banquet done, these Masquers came in with six gentlemen disguised in silk, bearing staff torches, and desired the ladies to dance.

The Masque evidently gave an opportunity to composers, dramatists and scenic artists to exercise their originality, especially as the money necessary for presenting Masques in an imposing fashion seems to have been readily forthcoming. One such Masque, *The Triumph of Peace*, compiled by James Shirley, included a great procession from Holborn to Whitehall, and the whole production cost twenty-one thousand pounds!

As might be expected, the Masque was not favoured by the Puritans, but it formed a prominent feature of musical life during the Restoration Period. English musicians at this time were in close touch with the development of the Opera in Italy and France, and the Masque required little alteration to make it conform to Opera. The latter was, however, not suited for outdoor performance and English operatic composers preferred that the dialogue should be spoken rather than sung in "Recitativo secco."

Henry Purcell. Fortunately there was in England a musical genius of pronounced originality who was able to turn to good account the interest shown by the public in dramatic productions in which music was lavishly introduced. This composer was Henry Purcell (1658-95). At an early age he became one of the Children of the Chapel Royal, and organist of Westminster Abbey in 1680. In his church music can be found striking passages which are in expressiveness far above anything so far produced. Cf. the passage from his Funeral Anthem given on the opposite page (the words accompanying this extract are "Deliver us not into the bitter pains of eternal death"). One does not often hear Purcell's anthems to-day except in cathedrals, as most of them are long and contain very ornate solos somewhat repugnant to modern taste. For much of his church music Purcell provided an orchestral accompaniment. During the latter part of his short life he was busy composing the Incidental Music for plays. In fact it was to Purcell that every dramatist first turned

Henry Purcell

when he wanted a musical colleague. His best operas
are *Dido and Æneas, King Arthur, Dioclesian* and *The
Indian Queen,* although in these music does not occupy
such a prominent place as in modern Opera. Some of
the songs in these operas, e.g. "Fairest Isle," "I attempt

from Love's sickness to fly," "When I am laid in earth," and "Come if you dare," have long been recognised as amongst the finest of old English songs.

Purcell's instrumental music for harpsichord and strings, especially "Sonatas for two violins, bass and harpsichord," is in attractiveness far above anything so far produced in that particular line. Of late, considerable interest in the works of Purcell has been aroused, and opportunities of hearing them are likely to become more frequent. Purcell's music is essentially English in its wholesome character and in its freedom from cheap sentiment and brooding over fancied grievances.[30] No better patriotic song than "Fairest Isle" could be desired, and no music is so likely to dispel "a fit of the blues" as "Nymphs and Shepherds."

From the death of Purcell until quite recently the musical historian seeks in vain to discover the names of any English composers who can be said to have been as influential as their greatest contemporaries on the Continent. But this statement must be qualified if we admit Handel to the company of English musicians.

The Instrumental Suite. When we compare the clavichord and harpsichord music of the late sixteenth century with that produced at the end of the seventeenth we do not find such great changes as those which are so marked in the sphere of vocal and orchestral music. The limited resources of these instruments were a great handicap; *legato* playing was practically impossible—a fatal defect from the point of view of expression.

---

[30] Record No. 118.

Nevertheless composers were gradually learning how to write harpsichord music less fragmentary in character than the very short dance tunes and Airs with Variations which formed the bulk of the music hitherto written for the instrument. Towards the end of the seventeenth century the musical form known as the "Suite" had become well established. These Suites generally consisted of a series of fairly short pieces, all in the same key and founded on dance-rhythms. A typical Suite for harpsichord would consist of a Prelude, followed by an Allemande (*moderato*), a Courante (*allegro*), a Minuet, a Sarabande (*andante,* in triple time), a Gavotte (*allegro moderato*) and a Gigue (*vivace*). Nearly all of these pieces comprised two distinct sections, beginning in a definite key, modulating towards a new key at the end of the first section and leading in the second section back to the original key. The subject-matter contained no violent contrasts; the character of the music was well-defined in the first few bars and maintained throughout. This scheme is known as "Binary Form," and it furnished the framework for most of the best harpsichord music.[31] Also, composers fully realised that the use of "accidentals" had destroyed the individuality of the Modes, and tended to reduce them to the types corresponding to our Major and Minor scales (see p. 66). The harpsichord was used in the orchestra during this period chiefly to play the "Continuo"; that is, while the other instruments were busy executing florid passages, the harpsichordist played the bass part together with the plain chords upon which the whole

---

[31] Records Nos. 8, 9, 10. Most of the Preludes in Bach's "Forty-eight" are in this form.

harmonic scheme was founded. (He was not, however, precluded from adding embellishments of his own.) The chords were indicated by a conventional series of figures; hence the term "figured bass." This use of the harpsichord extended well into the eighteenth century, and it was also applied to organ accompaniment. The most interesting music written for the harpsichord up to the time of Bach was the work of the Frenchman Couperin. He adopted the plan of giving fanciful titles to his little tunes which would more or less indicate the character of the music; e.g. "Les petits moulins a vent," "La poule," etc. (Cf. Records Nos. D 644; 05567; D 490.)

Chamber Music and Concerto. Apart from the orchestra, more and more use came to be made of combinations of instruments which would be effective in an ordinary room; e.g. viols and other stringed instruments in conjunction with the harpsichord.[32] Purcell's *Ten Sonatas for two violins, bass viol and harpsichord* already referred to are very good specimens of Chamber Music. By the end of the century, instruments of the violin family had been so much improved that their superiority over all other stringed instruments could not be denied. The Italian, Corelli, was the first great solo violinist; he found out what types of music are and are not effective on this instrument,[33] and his success encouraged the rapid development of violin-playing so noticeable during this period.

Brief mention must be made of the "Concerto,"

[32] Record No. 12.

[33] Records Nos. 13 to 17.

which begins to take definite shape at the end of the seventeenth century. Every band would possess some players more skilled than others; and it is only natural to find that composers recognised the fact by writing music with an elaborate part for one or more soloists, while the rest of the band played a comparatively simple accompaniment. The Concerto in the hands of the great classical composers has been developed to such an extent that it is recognised as one of the most pregnant of musical Forms.[34]

[34] Records Nos. 35, 36, 37.

CHAPTER XIII

HANDEL AND BACH

THE musical historian who within a limited space desires to trace the development of music from the eighteenth century onwards is confronted with a difficult task. The amount of really good music produced by a host of able composers is bewildering; and all that can be done is to select and discuss works which are either the best examples of established forms, or which reveal an effort to create something new. A great deal of music is purely imitative: it merely adds to the bulk, and does not break any new ground. Such music has only a brief existence, and no good purpose would be served by compiling a catalogue of works which are entirely forgotten. Hence it will be necessary in this brief outline to omit the names of many composers who were of considerable eminence in their time, and to concentrate on a few whose work is of special significance.

In the first half of the eighteenth century two names—Handel and Bach—eclipse all others. The contrast between the life and works of these two musical giants is remarkable. Both were born in Germany in the same year—1685. They never met, although they knew something of each other's doings. As will be seen, their respective careers were very different. Handel in his later years became the idol of the British musical public and died a wealthy man. Bach was widely known as a remarkably accomplished organist, but as a composer was hardly recognised outside the town of Leipzig, where he spent the last uneventful years of his life as musical director ("Cantor") of the principal churches of that town. Handel lived in the limelight; Bach passed his existence in the comparative obscurity of a provincial town, and not until he had been dead for a hundred years was his real genius widely recognised.

Handel. Handel adopted a musical career much against the wishes of his parents. His great gifts were, however, recognised by the Duke of Weissenfels; at his persuasion the boy was placed under the care of the celebrated organist Zachau, who helped him to become familiar with the best musical works available. He then obtained a post as violinist at the Opera House of Hamburg, which was at that time the centre of German musical activity. Here he produced his first Opera on the usual pattern. After a short visit to Italy in 1706, where he found that he could hold his own with the best Italian operatic composers, he returned to Germany and became "Kapellmeister," i.e. chief court-musician, to the Elector of Saxony, who afterwards became George I of England. Handel visited England in 1710, produced an Opera—*Rinaldo*—with much success, and in 1718 settled permanently in this country. For three years he was chapel-master to the Duke of Chandos and had a good orchestra and choir at his disposal.

After this he became involved in operatic enterprises which brought him to bankruptcy. Opera in England was entirely under Italian influence and remained so for many years. But a different type of Opera ("Ballad Opera") which took the form of a comedy liberally interspersed with familiar ditties—often in a garbled version—became fashionable. Gay's *Beggar's Opera* is the best specimen.

The writing of Operas was not then a very exacting task: little was necessary but the ability to write Arias which would give celebrated singers an opportunity to exhibit their prowess, to connect these Arias with "Recitativo secco" and to add a conventional orchestral accompaniment. An industrious composer could turn out an opera in two or three weeks. Handel's operas had a short life, and are valuable to us chiefly on account of some beautiful Arias of a simple character. It was not until Handel was fifty-five years old that he undertook the enterprise which secured for him so high a place in the favour of the British public. He had already written one or two oratorios in the conventional style, which aroused some interest. It occurred to him that as Opera in England was in a bad way, it might be well to discover whether Oratorio on a large scale would prove attractive. The experiment succeeded and thenceforth Handel confined his efforts to Oratorio. The list of his oratorios is a long one, comprising *Saul, Messiah, Judas Maccabeus, Israel in Egypt, Samson,* and several others.

Handel's Oratorios. The outstanding feature in these works is the prominence given to the Chorus. Hitherto, both in Opera and Oratorio the place of honour had been taken by the Aria; the expansive and majestic choruses of Handel provided a new experience for the musical public and they approved it wholeheartedly. No pains were spared in order to secure adequate performances; these were profitable both artistically and financially. For the last few years of his life Handel was blind; curiously enough, he was operated upon by the same oculist who had treated Bach just as unsuccessfully. Handel's operas are not very remarkable, and his instrumental works, apart from his Organ Concertos, are not important; his fame rests almost entirely upon his oratorios. Of these, only a very few are regularly performed.

There must be weighty reasons for Handel's long-continued popularity. In the first place he recognised that there is an essential difference between a good vocal and a good instrumental style. Some modern writers overlook this fact and treat the voices as instruments, so that the vocalists are asked to sing music which is difficult and ungrateful. Even when the technical difficulties are mastered, the audience is more bewildered than impressed. Handel was seldom a sinner in this respect; Bach, however, cannot be acquitted of the fault. Take such a well-known chorus as "And the glory of the Lord" (*Messiah*).[35] Even an inefficient choir can make something of this and can enjoy making the attempt. The musical material is of the very slightest; the accompaniment is practically a duplication of the voice-parts, and there is very little variety of any kind. Yet this chorus is extraordinarily effective. Again, the

[35] Record C/1044 (H.M.V.).

brief Recitative "Thy rebuke hath broken his heart" (*Messiah*), which on paper looks almost meagre, is a perfect expression in musical terms of the deepest dejection. It is hardly necessary to cite the "Dead March" in *Saul* as another wonderful example of a great effect obtained by simple means. Handel never obscures his main themes with subordinate details which the average hearer will not detect; every note tells. Thus it is easy to listen to Handel; one can with little effort hear all that he wants us to hear. He is like a painter who paints quickly on a big canvas with a big brush, ignoring all details not essential to the general scheme.

It is a pity that Handel, like most of the composers of the period, was too often satisfied with wretched librettos which a modern audience cannot listen to with patience. Indeed, it may be said that it is the lack of good librettos which is largely responsible for the decline of Oratorio in late years. Mendelssohn's *Elijah* and Elgar's *Dream of Gerontius* are not handicapped in this respect.

Bach. Whereas the number of works by Handel which are regularly performed has diminished, the opposite is the case with Bach, since 1830 at any rate. The reason of this will be seen presently. The essential details of Bach's career can soon be recounted. For generations the Bach family had been prominent in the musical life of Germany. It was assumed as a matter of course that a Bach would follow in his father's steps and become a professional musician. Johann Sebastian Bach, the greatest of all musicians, went through the usual preliminary training and soon became widely

JOHANN SEBASTIAN BACH

known as an accomplished organist. The chief posts held by him were at Weimar (chief musician at the Ducal court), Arnstadt (organist), Cöthen (Kapellmeister) and Leipzig (Cantor). At Weimar, and later at Cöthen, he had opportunities of becoming acquainted with orchestral works, while at Arnstadt and at Leipzig music for the church claimed most of his attention. Opera did not attract him in the least. At Leipzig, where he spent the last twenty-seven years of his life, he was kept very busy with the composition and rehearsal of music required by the churches whose musical affairs were entrusted to him; what spare time he had was largely devoted to the careful revision of his early instrumental works. Although never in actual want, he accumulated no fortune, and soon after his death his wife was obliged to ask for "parish relief." He never sought to advertise himself; only a very few of his compositions were published until he had been dead a hundred years. He seems to have taken little interest in the preservation of the scores of most of his works after the first two or three performances, and it is no thanks to him that we possess so many of the original mss. and authentic copies of his best compositions. Bach's influence on his contemporaries was consequently almost negligible.

Now such an uneventful career hardly seems to square with Bach's reputation as "the Father of Music." Yet he, in his works, sums up all that had been slowly materialising in preceding centuries. E.g., hundreds of Fugues had been written before his time; but he wrote better Fugues than have been written before or since.[36] Passion Music was no novelty; in fact, nearly all the striking features of Bach's *Matthew Passion* can be paralleled in earlier settings; yet by general consent this work remains supreme in its own class. The Choral Prelude was a well-established form long before Bach; but his compositions remain the finest specimens in that form. The same may be said of the Church Cantatas. Bach was no innovator; he took music as he found it—and improved it. No higher tribute could be paid to him than the statement of the fact that a professional musician tired, and possibly bored, nearly always turns to Bach for solace.

Bach's style. It is not easy to indicate, in a way which the amateur will understand, the particular qualities which make Bach's music of such supreme interest to the cultured musician. Everybody feels, more or less, the spell of the *Matthew Passion* and the *Mass in B minor,* but many of his works are so complex that the average listener is confused. They depend for their effect very largely upon intricate counterpoint, and only a minority even of musical folk can appreciate this. Often, with Bach, one can hardly "see the wood for the trees"; Handel takes good care to make the trees inconspicuous. Then, again, musical phraseology in Bach's time was very different from that of the nineteenth and twentieth centuries. In these days one expects strong contrasts, glowing colour and violent climaxes, otherwise a work is dubbed monotonous. In a piece by Bach we usually find that the general style is set in the first few bars and adhered to throughout. His Arias are

[36] Record No. 10.

mostly constructed entirely from a few short phrases announced in the Introduction; these are afterwards distributed impartially between voice and orchestra and new matter is seldom introduced. With the Italian masters, Handel included, the Aria was regarded as a vocal melody with an orchestral accompaniment, the voice part being all-important. But Bach generally treats the vocal melody as being only one of a number of melodies; the voice part is of no more importance than the others. This makes considerable demands upon both singer and audience. Again, he assumed that in the choruses the instrumental forces would be at least as powerful as the choral.

Here is a typical passage from one of the Church Cantatas. It is obvious that we have here not a vocal solo with accompaniment, but the voice part is only one of five streams of melody, all of which are equally significant.

Bach's finest vocal works on a large scale—excluding the Church Cantatas, of which we possess no fewer than two hundred and six—are the *B minor Mass* (the greatest of all musical works on a sacred subject), and the *Matthew Passion*. The latter (see p. 119) is partly dramatic, partly reflective and devotional, and is quite out of place in a Concert Hall. The *Mass* was not composed for use in Church—it is much too long and complicated for such a purpose. Of Bach's works for keyboard instruments it need only be said here that many of them belong to that category of compositions which affords rather more pleasure to the performer than to the listener; this, however, is no demerit. But

Praise —— O — Zi - on, praise — God, praise   O

praise Thy God with glad —— ——— ——— ness.

what has been said above is not sufficient to account for the esteem in which Bach is held by all competent critics. It has been asserted that "Bach was the first to subordinate musical technique to *expression*"; this statement will perhaps be more intelligible to the student after he has read the next chapter.

CHAPTER XIV

FORM AND EXPRESSION

Vocal Form. We have now arrived at a period when experiments in writing long instrumental works assumed great importance. As regards instrumental music especially, the question of Form or Design is a matter of great moment. If a composer proposes to write a vocal work, the design which ought to be adopted is to some extent obvious. E.g. suppose he is going to provide a musical setting for *Kyrie eleison, Christe eleison, Kyrie eleison* to be used in church. Clearly, many problems in Form are here decided for him. The music must be devotional in character, without strong contrasts and of reasonable length. Moreover there are three distinct sections, and the text suggests that the music for *Christe eleison* will be somewhat different, but not greatly so, from that of the other sections; also, that the last section will be set substantially to the same music as the first. Indeed, in setting any poem to music, the construction of the poem itself will settle many questions; e.g. the length of phrases, position of the climaxes, repetition of sections, and so forth. In the case of a hymn-tune the form is so circumscribed by custom and necessity that the composer has little choice in the matter.

Instrumental Form. But with purely instrumental music none of these limitations holds; the composer is free to cast his musical ideas into any shape he likes; but this means that he will have to use his judgment in selecting from the mass of material that which will be best adapted for his particular purpose. Is the work to be long or short? Is it to be uniformly lively or solemn, or are there to be strong contrasts? In what order are the themes to be presented and how are they to be dealt with? If it is an orchestral work, of what instruments is the band to consist? All these and many more questions have to be decided before actual composition begins.[37] Now even the simplest instrumental piece, if it is to agree with our instinctive notions of what is, and what is not, musically satisfactory, has to conform to some design or other; a mere rigmarole of disconnected phrases makes no appeal. Moreover, the fact that musical sounds are fugitive, and that memory is necessary to hold together the sounds which, as it were, pass before us in a long procession, demands that the design of the whole must be quite clear. The most important fact to bear in mind is that *repetition* of some kind lies at the very root of Form. Call to mind any large building which is generally agreed to be architecturally beautiful, and notice what a large part repetition of certain features plays in the whole structure. So in the case of instrumental music in particular; repetition of accent, rhythmic groups, melodic phrases, harmonic progressions, climaxes, and

[37] Anyone who wishes to realise even in a slight degree the importance of form should ask himself: "Suppose that I am requested to write a simple piece for pianoforte, (no other stipulation being given), how should I set about it?"

so forth, cannot be left to chance. Besides, care has to be taken lest repetition should degenerate into monotony. Then the opposite feature to repetition, viz. contrast, has to be considered in all its bearings; and the necessity of a due balance being maintained between repetition and contrast demands attention. Too frequent repetition leads to boredom; too much contrast to restlessness.

In course of time, composers by dint of much experiment have devised certain musical forms, i.e. types of musical architecture, which when skilfully used will ensure that the music will commend itself to the musical judgment of listeners. The most prominent of these forms are briefly explained in Appendix III; what concerns us here is that in the eighteenth century certain schemes came to be recognised as especially suitable for long instrumental works. The old Suites, as perfected by Bach, can hardly be included in this category, as they really consisted of a collection of short pieces with very little connection between them. In other words, the Suite is deficient in so far that the principle of *unity* is not very evident therein. A number of small buns does not constitute a cake. But meanwhile Corelli (*b.* 1653) and his contemporaries had worked out a scheme which proved especially suitable for violin music, with simple accompaniment for the harpsichord.[38] Compositions of this type were called *Sonate da Camera,* or, if particularly serious, *Sonate da Chiesa.* Such works were generally modelled on this plan: *(a)* a dignified introduction, *(b)* an allegro movement, *(c)* a slow movement, followed by *(d)* a

[38] Record No. 13.

brilliant Finale. This form differed from the Suite, in that the separate sections were not necessarily founded on dance-forms. We find examples of this primitive Sonata form in the works of Bach, and more frequently amongst the compositions of his son, Philip Emmanuel. But the first composer really to solve the problem presented by instrumental music—other than that for the organ—was Joseph Haydn.

Haydn. Haydn was born in 1732, when Bach and Handel were forty-seven years of age. He was born under a lucky star; only in his early days did he feel the pinch of poverty; thereafter he always found wealthy patrons who made things easy for him. From 1766 to 1790 he was musical director of a large musical establishment set up by Prince Esterhazy at his palatial residence not very far from Vienna, which had now become the centre of musical life. Here Haydn had at his disposal an Opera house, a fine band and a good choir. Hence his natural genius had full scope for development. Apparently he did not take Opera seriously, but preferred to experiment with chamber-music, i.e. music for a very small band (the string-quartet by preference[39]) and for the orchestra. He soon became recognised by the world outside as a great composer, and his duties at the Court did not prevent him from keeping in touch with musical activities. In 1791 he visited London, where he was rapturously received. A second visit in 1794 was even more successful; his Symphonies, especially, made a great impression. Soon after his return to Vienna he composed his oratorio *The Creation,* which, in spite of

[39] Record No. 19, also D 1443 and 1444 (Col.).

its ridiculous libretto, was received with enthusiasm and performed by all the best choirs in Europe. This work remains one of the very few classical oratorios which have not fallen into oblivion.

Haydn and the Orchestra. In 1792 Beethoven became a rather restless pupil of Haydn's. Mozart was also a contemporary, and Haydn generously recognised the genius of both. Composition came easily to Haydn; in addition to his vocal works and chamber-music he wrote no fewer than one hundred and twenty-five Symphonies for orchestra, and it is these upon which his fame principally depends. He is often referred to as the "Father of instrumental music." This is because, through his exertions, orchestral music as an independent art-form competed successfully with vocal music, including Opera and Oratorio. The orchestra itself, on account of the great improvements which had been made in the manufacture of instruments, was now a much more pliable body, capable of giving expression to great musical ideas. The bowed instruments were now regarded as by far the best foundation for the orchestra. The wind instruments, too, had been considerably improved and the coarse tone and uncertain intonation largely mitigated. In fact, before Haydn's death the orchestra had been organised on a basis which, broadly speaking, is still retained.

Sonata Form. Let us see how Haydn solved the problem presented by the composition of long instrumental works. He did not actually *invent* "Sonata Form,"[40] but proved in a practical fashion that this

[40] A Symphony is practically a Sonata written for full

answered all reasonable requirements. A typical Haydn Symphony or Sonata is constructed on some such plan as this:

(1) A short slow Introduction (sometimes omitted);

(2) An *allegro* movement in Sonata Form;

(3) A slow movement;

(4) A Minuet;

(5) A Rondo, or a lively movement in Sonata Form. (Many modifications of Sonata Form are possible and effective.)

This method of planning out a long instrumental work proved eminently satisfactory, and has been followed more or less strictly by all the great classical and by many modern composers. It is suited to chamber-music as well as orchestral, and provides a framework fitted no less for the expression of the gaiety characteristic of most of Haydn's works than for the profound musical ideas of Beethoven.

Mozart. Wolfgang Amadeus Mozart was born twenty-four years after Haydn and died at the early age of thirty-five. His brain developed at an abnormal rate, and this development took the form of an extraordinary sensitiveness to musical sounds. His father trained him judiciously, and at the age of six he was "on tour" with

---

orchestra. The term "Sonata Form" is sometimes applied to the work as a whole; sometimes to the conventional design used for the first movement—but not exclusively so. To avoid confusion, we shall retain the term "Sonata Form" only in the first sense; otherwise we shall speak of "Modern Binary Form." (See Appendix III.)

his sister, giving concerts in various musical centres. London was visited in 1764, while the next thirteen years were spent by Mozart in travelling and composing, although Salzburg in the Tyrol was his headquarters. He became a most prolific composer in nearly every branch of music then in vogue, and was regarded by competent critics such as Haydn as the greatest musician of the age. Although he had little difficulty in bringing his works to a hearing, he received a very small monetary reward for them. In those days it was not the composer who waxed rich on the profits of a successful opera, but the producer. "Performing royalties" were not legally enforceable. Though there were many wealthy patrons of music ready to give Mozart unstinted praise, they stopped at that. He was often in actual want, partly owing to his poor business instincts and partly the result of an unfortunate marriage, and he was buried in a pauper's grave.

An enumeration of really important compositions by Mozart—works which are still performed and regarded as master-works would take up too much space here. Perhaps at the head of the list would come the four great operas written in Vienna, viz. *Seraglio, Figaro, Don Giovanni* and *Die Zauberflöte (The Magic Flute)*. Amongst his choral works the *Requiem* stands supreme, and his four last Symphonies, especially the *G minor* and *Jupiter* Symphonies, still possess a fascination which is not likely to wane. His works for keyboard instruments are not important. Mozart's standpoint with regard to musical expression as stated by himself is interesting: "Passion, whether great or not, must never be expressed in an exaggerated manner, and Music—even in the most harrowing moment—ought never to offend the ear, but should always remain Music, which desires to give pleasure." In the sphere of chamber-music he was easily the greatest writer before Beethoven.

Mozart's Style. It is not easy to explain the peculiar merits of Mozart; one feels them, but they are too subtle to describe in cold print. He had no revolutionary ideas; but, like Bach, he took musical forms pretty much as he found them. An amateur would not find it easy to decide whether a particular string-quartet was by Haydn or Mozart. However, more than his contemporaries he found in music a means of expressing ideas of great significance. (See the opening of the development section of the first movement, and the whole of the Finale of the *G minor Symphony.*) Mozart's extreme natural sensitiveness to musical sounds prevented him from writing anything cheap or ugly; one need only refer to the delicate orchestral accompaniments in the operas. This sensitiveness demands a corresponding care on the part of performers of his music. Anything like a slipshod performance makes Mozart's finest movements sound trivial. Every note, and still more every rest, must be carefully considered in relation to what precedes and follows. The consequence of this is that no fair judgment on Mozart can be passed until one has heard his works performed by real artists.[41] One may apply to him the remark approved by all painters with regard to Velasquez, "Everything he does is right." It is

[41] Records Nos. 20, 43, 71.

worthy of note that even the most advanced of modern musicians confess that they still find inspiration from the works of Mozart.

Expression. It is necessary at this stage to try to understand a term which must continually recur, viz. "Expression." Music may be regarded from two points of view—the "decorative" and the "expressive." A composer may possibly have no other intention than that of presenting music beautiful to listen to; or he may wish to make use of music as a means of communicating his feelings or ideas to others. In the first case, he may be said to lay most stress on the "decorative," in the other on the "expressive," aspect of music. Much of the instrumental music of the eighteenth century is almost purely decorative; there is nothing to say about it except that it appeals to one's sense of beauty. The composer strove for "a concourse of sweet sounds," and was satisfied with that. But often one feels that he is impelled by an additional motive; he is under the stress of emotion, and wishes us to share this.

Ordinary speech is by no means capable of communicating the nature of all our feelings to another person. Everybody recognises this. One may say "I feel sad, jolly, puzzled," and so forth, but only a very few mental states can be described in ordinary language. One constantly meets with such phrases as "Words fail to tell . . . "; "I can't describe it exactly . . . "; "He was so overcome that he could say nothing"; "I feel so-so." Of course, speech can be eked out by gesture-language— probably the most primitive form of speech. One may *look* happy, active, or miserable: facial expression in particular is a very effective method of communicating one's feelings, as every singer knows.

It is a matter of common experience that some music can take us "out of ourselves," i.e. can arouse feelings which are not stirred by the ordinary events of the day, and which cannot be described in every-day speech. "Decorative" music can do this, but the feelings it arouses are mostly those of pleasure and satisfaction only. [Notice that the "decorative" and "expressive" aspects of music do not absolutely exclude one another; it is a question of which element predominates.] The former aspect is concerned mainly with *beauty of sound;* "expressive" music may comprise very ugly sounds. Composers of the eighteenth century had so far profited by the experiments of their numerous predecessors that they had a much larger musical vocabulary for the communication of their ideas. Every composer has to go for most of his material, e.g. rhythm, melody and chords, etc., to the works of the past, unless indeed he is an out-and-out revolutionary. The new material contributed by any one composer is only small in amount, but the combined efforts of the composers since the time of Palestrina had resulted in a large amount of musical material lying ready to hand, waiting to be recast into new forms. If a composer wished to express his emotions he was now better able to do so; he was familiar with many varied rhythms, progressions of chords, modulations and so forth, out of which he could pick and choose. Moreover, for a composer of the latter part of the eighteenth century it was no longer necessary to waste time in experiments which had already been tried and found wanting; should he decide, for instance, to cast his ideas, conceived on a large scale, into an instrumental mould, Sonata Form as perfected by Haydn and Mozart was found elastic and adequate enough for such a purpose.

CHAPTER XV

BEETHOVEN

TOWARDS the end of the eighteenth century a general spirit of unrest was noticeable. A feeling was abroad that there was something wrong with the world; that the great gulf which separated the life of the rich and powerful from that of the less fortunate class ought to be narrowed; that the ideals of Freedom, Brotherhood and Equality, if put into practice, would result in greater happiness and prosperity. The more honourable of the leaders of the French Revolution held firmly to these ideals, although events proved that they were not easily attained. Nevertheless, men's minds were very active; speculation and experiment were applied freely to all branches of knowledge. It is only necessary to mention such names as Rousseau, Kant, Hegel, Shelley, Goethe and George Washington to prove the truth of this remark.

Beethoven's career. It was hardly likely that music would not be influenced by this new spirit, and it was Beethoven who did for music what was done by such eminent men as those named above in their special spheres of work. The details of the life of this great musician are not exciting. He was born at Bonn in 1770. His father, a ne'er-do-well, tried, with small success, to persuade the public that his son was a prodigy. The latter really began his musical career as a member of a theatrical orchestra. In 1787 he visited Vienna, and had a few lessons from Mozart. Five years later he became acquainted with Haydn, and this meeting resulted in his becoming Haydn's pupil. But already Beethoven was composing music of a novel kind which the old master found unintelligible. The musical public of Vienna, however, welcomed it, and Beethoven thenceforward made his headquarters in that city. In 1798 he realised that the greatest misfortune which could happen to a musician, namely deafness, was coming upon him. He was by nature solitary and irritable, and it is not to be wondered at that he had many grievances, fancied or real. Yet long before his death in 1827 he was regarded not only in Vienna but also throughout Europe as the greatest musical genius of his time; and he found no difficulty in getting his works performed and published.

Methods of Work. Beethoven was one of the world's greatest men; it was chance that made it natural for him to express himself in music rather than in any other art or science. What we know of his life proves that he felt very deeply; to put it rather crudely, when he was angry he was very angry; if happy, he was boisterous; if annoyed, he flew into a violent rage. Composition was for him no easy task. Such utterances as these: "I will grapple with fate; it shall never drag me down"; "I live only in my music"; "I am quite hoarse with stamping and swearing"; show at what high pressure he was living.

LUDWIG VAN BEETHOVEN

From one who knew him in 1826, when he was living with his brother at the small village of Gneixendorf, we have a vivid account of his habits. "At 5.30 a.m. he would be up and at his table, beating time with hands and feet, singing, humming and writing. At 7.30 was the family breakfast, and directly after it he hurried out of doors, and would saunter about the fields, calling out, waving his hands, going now very slowly, then very fast, and then suddenly standing still and writing in a kind of pocket-book." We still have many of these "pocket-books," and from them can see how much labour it cost him to compose and revise what seems at first sight a very simple tune. No great composer ever took so much trouble over the invention of a melody, but then no composer could make so effective a use of a tune when he had got it to his satisfaction. Observe for example how much Beethoven could express with a little tune consisting only of the first four notes of a descending scale in the first movement of the *Pianoforte Sonata in D major* (Op. 10, No. 3), or with a simple arpeggio as in the first movement of the *Sonata Appassionata*. It is in this direction that his greatness is conspicuous. Nearly everybody can invent tunes, but how to weld these together, so as to convey the idea of unity, how to present them in the most effective manner, how to deal with them so that they suggest much more than is apparent at first sight, how to use them as the text of a musical sermon which becomes more impressive each time it is delivered—this is the difficult task which Beethoven undertook so successfully. If long life is a test of the value of any work of art, the best of his works come well out of the ordeal. For more than a century they have stood at the head of the repertoire of all respectable orchestras; the *C minor Symphony* has been played more often than any other composition of its class.

Whilst Beethoven generally adopted "Sonata Form" for his instrumental works, he used this very freely. Sometimes he placed the slow movement first, as in the *Moonlight Sonata;* occasionally he begins with an "Air with Variations," or replaces the staid Minuet by a lively "Scherzo." The last movement of the *Choral Symphony* is really an Air elaborately laid out for the orchestra, with Variations for a chorus.

"Expression" in Beethoven's works. It is customary to divide Beethoven's musical career into three periods: (1) the period in which he wrote works very similar to those of Haydn and Mozart; (2) that in which the framework employed is much more elastic and the musical ideas are more suggestive and impressive (the majority of his most popular works belong to this period); (3) the latest period, in which he tried to express thoughts to which no one so far had succeeded in giving utterance. He wrote only one opera, *Fidelio,* and with the exception of the *Mass in D*—a gigantic work for the concert-room—his vocal music is not of the greatest importance. Some notion of the wide range of emotion which he expressed in his music may be gained by reference to the following examples. (The *predominant* mood alone is indicated.)

Piano Sonata, Op. 10, No. 3 (Slow movement)	*Solemnity*
Symphony No. 2 (Slow movement) ...	*Happy content*
Many Scherzos from the Sonatas ...	*Whimsicality*
Symphony No. 9 (Third movement) ...	*Titanic force*
Symphony No. 5 (First movement)[1] ...	*"I will grapple with fate"*
„ „ (Bridge-passage, leading from Scherzo to Finale)	*Mystery*
"Gloria" of Mass in D	*Religious exaltation*
Symphony No. 7 (Last movement) ...	*Boisterous energy*
Overture "Coriolan"	*Determination*
Symphony No. 8 (Finale)	*Fun*

Such a list as this might be extended almost indefinitely. There is hardly any emotion to which mankind is prone that has not its counterpart in the music of Beethoven.

CHAPTER XVI

SCHUBERT—ROMANTICISM

BEETHOVEN'S triumphs, notable as they were, did not cover the whole field of music. Some important types of the art, although perfectly familiar to us to-day, were hardly touched upon by him. E.g. the solo-song with pianoforte accompaniment—a musical form now almost too well known—had not been treated very seriously by any of the classical composers. Haydn and Mozart had merely dabbled in song-writing, and Beethoven left only a few examples. A vocalist who wished to exhibit his prowess on the concert-platform was practically driven to select an Aria from some Opera or Oratorio. The first really great composer to convince the musical world that the art of setting lyrics to music was worth cultivation was Franz Schubert, next to Mozart probably the most remarkable natural musical genius the world has ever known. His brain was teeming with melody; unlike Beethoven he composed with tremendous rapidity and apparently with little effort. His general education was very imperfect, but the command of musical resources which most other composers obtained only by long and severe study came to him almost too easily.

Schubert's career. Schubert was born at Vienna in 1797 in very humble circumstances. As a boy in the "Convict" school, where choristers were trained for the Court Chapel, he obtained some help in his musical studies, and at the age of thirteen was composing quite respectable music. He soon showed facility in song-writing and by the time he was nineteen years old had produced songs superior to any that had so far appeared.[42] But his circle of acquaintance was small, and he was utterly devoid of "push." Vienna at that time was too much interested in Beethoven to bestow any attention on a poor assistant schoolmaster. However, amongst his friends were a few discerning musicians who gave semi-private renderings of his shorter works, especially songs and chamber-music. Thus encouraged, he continued to write at express speed: in one year— 1815—he wrote 146 songs, besides three operas, two Masses and many instrumental works, including three symphonies. Slowly it began to dawn on the Viennese public that they had a great song-writer in their midst, and publishers ventured to issue some of the songs, for which, however, Schubert was paid a mere pittance. Beethoven cordially expressed his admiration, but offered him no further help. His personality was not such as to win for him influential friends who would see to it that he received the rewards due to him, but this did not deter him from trying his hand at nearly every branch of musical composition. Just as his fortunes were beginning to mend he caught typhoid fever and died at the early age of 31. Only a small proportion

[42] Record No. 122.

of the tremendous number of his compositions was performed or published in his lifetime.

His Songs. While Schubert wrote several instrumental works which still live, including some splendid chamber-music,[43] it is by virtue of his skill in song-writing that he holds such an important position in musical history. A large number of these are so familiar to us that they may be called "household words" in music. Only a few can be mentioned here: "The Erl-King," "Hark! the lark,"[44] "Who is Sylvia?" "The Young Nun," "Serenade," "Trust in Spring," and the two song-cycles "The Miller's Daughter" and "The Winter Journey." In these songs we find a feature not common hitherto, but henceforward to assume great importance, viz. an equal division of interest between the vocal and instrumental parts. The accompaniment is no longer merely a support for the voice, but helps materially to create a mood corresponding to the sentiment of the poem. In fact, we have not a solo-song with accompaniment, but rather a duet for voice and pianoforte. Noteworthy examples are "The Erl-King,"[45] "The Young Nun," "The Organ Grinder," and "To Music."

The "Unfinished Symphony." From the point of view of musical progress the most important instrumental work of Schubert is the *Unfinished Symphony.*[46] This

[43] Record No. 25.

[44] Record No. 2/3241 (H.M.V.).

[45] Record No. 122.

[46] Record No. 40.

work may be regarded as a perfect example of musical "Romanticism." The term "Romantic" may be regarded as the opposite of "matter-of-fact." The literature of the Middle Ages comprised a large number of romances, i.e. tales of chivalry, fairy-stories and legends which dealt with events and situations that can have existed only in the imagination: in fact, the supernatural element was prominent. We meet with this feature, of course, in Shakespeare's *A Midsummer-Night's Dream* and in *The Tempest*. Such romances introduced the element of "other-worldliness" and mystery. Towards the end of the eighteenth century a strong revival of interest in the old romances was noticeable, and many writers took these as a model for their contributions to literature. Whilst no art remained unaffected by the new spirit, its influence was strongly felt in music.

Weber and German Opera. The trouble with Opera had always been in connection with the libretto or plot. In the finest Italian operas the music was far and away better than the words; e.g. it was hardly likely that a German audience would be greatly thrilled by a story based on the more or less disreputable love-affairs of Italian grandees. The Romanticists thought that a way out of the difficulty could be found by taking a play founded on the characteristics of the old romances. The first operatic composer to prove that this was a sound principle was Weber. In *Der Freischütz*[47] he used a libretto based on a German story; and this strongly appealed to German audiences, who at that time were beginning to be affected by the spirit of nationalism

[47] Record No. 46.

which afterwards so strongly influenced the course of European history. The opening section of the well-known overture to *Der Freischütz* illustrates at once the new principle which was soon afterwards adopted by many composers, notably by Richard Wagner. Obviously, music that was to succeed in suggesting the supernatural could not be matter-of-fact; hence composers had to exercise their imagination and originality in thinking out new progressions of harmony, orchestration, and so forth; in fact they had to extend the musical vocabulary. Of course, many operas continued to be written which can hardly be described as "Romantic"; indeed many modern operas cannot be thus labelled, but the newer methods influenced all forms of composition, and the range of musical expression was widely expanded.

Romanticism. But what about Romanticism in the case of music without words or action? For instance, it is easy for an audience to get the notion of fairy-land when the words sung are all about fairies and these beings presumably appear on the stage. Instrumental music by itself cannot successfully illustrate; it can only stimulate the formation of mental images. But there are many examples of instrumental music which have all the qualities of Romance—mystery, "other-worldliness," weirdness, and so forth. In speaking about Schubert's *Unfinished Symphony*[48] it is not necessary to suppose that the composer deliberately set out to write a Romantic work; but, all the same, this Symphony has many of the distinguishing features which we associate with Romanticism. The sombre and mysterious phrase

[48] Record No. 40.

announced at the outset by the basses *pp* excites the imagination at once; evidently the movement is going to be anything but commonplace; it may even suggest that a tragic story is to be unfolded. The second theme is more comforting, but soon the ominous first subject reappears; it is dissected[49], and the fragments are hurled almost defiantly by the full orchestra, so that even the dullest listener cannot help feeling that a tragedy is suggested. Perhaps the abrupt changes of key at the end of the second movement are still more arresting in a different way. For a perfect musical expression of "mystery" cf. Chopin's *Prelude No. 2* for pianoforte.

[49] See pp. 209, 210.

CHAPTER XVII

BERLIOZ—"PROGRAMME MUSIC"

THERE are many composers whose chief claim to eminence is not that they created even a small revolution in the musical world, but that they added to musical literature some more excellent examples based on forms which were already well established. Hence such writers as Cherubini, Spohr, Gounod, Raff and many other composers of high rank will receive mention only in particular connections.

Berlioz. But the first few years of the nineteenth century saw the birth of several composers who really contributed something novel. Foremost amongst these were Berlioz (a Frenchman), Chopin (a native of Poland), and Schumann (a German). Berlioz (1803-69) was a stormy petrel in the musical world. He was a man with very big ideas, many of them quite impracticable. He was the first composer of note consistently to introduce into his instrumental works the dramatic element; i.e. he had in his mind a story or series of situations around which the music was written. This will be explained more fully below; meanwhile notice that it involves much modification of "Sonata Form." But in another direction Berlioz did work which was of the utmost value to his successors, viz. in connection with the orchestra. He made a deep study of the peculiarities of every orchestral instrument, and showed that there were possibilities of new combinations and novel effects which previous composers had never suspected. His *Treatise on Instrumentation* still remains a standard work on the subject, and his own compositions reveal the value of his discoveries, which were annexed by his successors—notably by Wagner. Unfortunately, Berlioz's principal works are not now often performed; he demands a very large (and expensive) orchestra, to say nothing of a big choir, and the works are too long drawn out for modern audiences. His jolly overture *Carnaval Romain,* however, is familiar enough.

Programme Music. The use by Berlioz of the dramatic element in instrumental music has already been mentioned; it is now necessary to explain a musical form which is the direct outcome of Berlioz's practice. This form is generally referred to by the term "Symphonic Poem." A composer in planning a long instrumental work may think only in terms of music—nothing in the shape of a story, plot, or "programme" need enter into his calculations. On the other hand, he may think of a story and try to illustrate it musically; it would, for instance, be quite easy to take the rhyme:

Jack and Jill went up the hill to fetch a pail of water;
Jack fell down and broke his crown, and Jill came tumbling after.

and write a short instrumental tune illustrating the catastrophe. An ascending scale passage, perhaps with a *rallentando,* followed by a downward scale ending with a *sforzando* would give us a crude "Symphonic Poem." (Observe that if the listener was not told previously that it was the story of "Jack and Jill" which the music was supposed to illustrate, he might interpret the tune quite otherwise.) The "programme" element can occasionally be met with in the works of the classical composers prior to Berlioz—e.g. the storm in Beethoven's *Sixth Symphony,* also his Pianoforte Sonata with the title *Departure, Absence, Return;* while hosts of lesser writers had composed little "picture-tunes." But it was Berlioz and Liszt who first applied this principle in a wholehearted fashion and helped to establish the "Symphonic Poem" as a musical form no less important than the Symphony.

As already intimated, musical language in general is very vague.[50] One may safely say that certain musical progressions, e.g. a trumpet-call, will suggest the same idea to everyone, but such phrases are only rarely met with in serious music. The second movement of Beethoven's *Piano Sonata in A flat* (Op. 26) would suggest to everybody a Funeral March, even if Beethoven had not given it that title. But when we take a long story in which, perhaps, we have to illustrate such ideas as "Love," "Peace," "Anger" and so forth, difficulties arise at once. A phrase which to one listener may suggest passion will to another suggest a headache. Let us see how Richard

---

[50] "Music has been called the language of nature, but it is a very imperfect language; it is all adjectives, and no substantives. It may represent certain qualities in objects, or raise similar affections in the mind to what these objects raise, but it cannot delineate the objects themselves."—*Dr Crotch.*

Strauss tries to get over the difficulty in his *Alpine Symphony* (this is really a Symphonic Poem). Sixty-one definite themes are used, and the music is divided into twenty-two sections beginning with " Night," " Sunrise," "Ascent," "Entry into the forest," "Ramble by the brook," and so on. These sections are numbered, and at the first London performance in 1923 cards were shown, as the music proceeded, on which the corresponding numbers were printed. Clearly this type of music is quite distinct from that of Mozart or Beethoven. The best Symphonic Poems such as *Don Quixote, Till Eulenspiegel's Merry Pranks, Don Juan, Death and Transfiguration, A Hero's Life* (all by Strauss[51]), *Hamlet* (Tschaikowsky) and *Falstaff* (Elgar) are acceptable because the music, apart from its connection with any story, is attractive. Many modern Concert-Overtures, i.e. orchestral pieces in one movement not belonging to an Opera, have a "programme" as the basis and are therefore small Symphonic Poems.

Chopin. We do not find as a rule that eminent composers are also brilliant performers. Neither is it of much use to go into raptures about the great executants of the past, since we have to rely entirely upon the opinions of those who heard them.[52] Of course they had an enormous influence on the progress of music; it would be useless for a composer to write brilliant music unless there were brilliant artists to perform it. Moreover, the fact that great artists were available

[51] Some of these are already recorded by H.M.V.

[52] The advent of the Gramophone and Piano-player has changed all that, so far as modern performers are concerned.

encouraged composers to give them something to do worthy of their high standing.

Liszt, Chopin and Mendelssohn, however, were fine pianists as well as composers. The pianoforte at the beginning of the nineteenth century had been so much improved that, except in volume of tone and sustaining power, it was little inferior to the pianoforte of to-day. It has been already said that every instrument has its limitations as well as its advantages. It was Chopin and Liszt who did for the pianoforte what Bach had done long before for the organ; they discovered the type of music which would be most effectively rendered on the pianoforte. Beethoven had by no means solved the problem, since many passages in his Sonatas are uncomfortable to play and would sound better on the orchestra. The pianoforte is specially adapted for rapid scale and arpeggio passages, which, if skilfully arranged, help to disguise the want of sustaining power in the instrument. But too many of the earlier composers were content to write showy passages of no musical interest whatever. It was Chopin who first discovered the great possibilities of effect which even a simple arpeggio possesses; this can be seen in many of his *Preludes* and *Studies,* and particularly well in the *G minor Ballade.*[53]

Short Works for Pianoforte. It is somewhat difficult to-day to realise how few short pianoforte solos of any real interest were available before the time of Chopin and Liszt. Schubert had written a few such pieces, e.g. *Moments Musicals* and the *Impromptus;* while John

---

[53] A large number of Chopin's works have been well recorded. Consult H.M.V. Catalogue.

Field had issued pieces of this type which he called *Nocturnes.* But no one has yet surpassed Chopin in this respect. He was a native of Poland, an intensely musical country possessing a large variety of dance-tunes—Valses, Polonaises, Mazurkas, etc. Taking these as a basis he wrote a large number of short works for the pianoforte, with which he fascinated the leaders of Parisian society who crowded the salons at which he played. Perhaps his most remarkable and original works are the *Preludes,* the *Studies,* the *Nocturnes,* and the four *Ballades;* these are still the "daily bread" of all pianists who can play them. The comparatively short pianoforte piece now became one of the most popular of musical forms, which even the most ambitious composer could not afford to neglect.

The "Leit-motif." The pianoforte works of Liszt are not very different from those of Chopin, except that they are too often spoilt by over-much repetition. Some of his most interesting works are exceedingly clever transcriptions for solo pianoforte or pianoforte duets of the great overtures, symphonies and songs.[54] But from our present point of view the most interesting feature in Liszt's original music is the frequent use of a device which is called "idée fixe," "leit-motif" or "leading theme." Berlioz also used it. It is the device that plays such an important part in the Symphonic Poem. The principle depends upon what is known in psychology as "the association of ideas." In this case we associate with a personage, event, mood, or emotion a characteristic phrase. Imagine, for instance, that

[54] Schubert's "Erl-King" e.g. (H.M.V. D 81).

one is writing a descriptive piece in which a certain character is supposed to appear and reappear. The obvious thing to do is to use the same musical phrase on his reappearance as on his first entry; in that way this "leading theme" would be associated with him, and at any time when we heard the phrase we should immediately have this personage in mind. Again, we can associate a particular musical phrase with a mood; e.g. we might invent a phrase illustrative of joy, and use it whenever *any* of the characters were supposed to be under the spell of this emotion; a further step still would be to employ a modified form of the *same* phrase (perhaps changing it from major to minor) when sorrow takes the place of joy. This explanation is rather crude, but may serve the purpose.

It is not at all difficult to transform a theme so as to illustrate several moods; e.g.

There is nothing really novel in this principle, but Berlioz and Liszt were the first to use it in a systematic way throughout a long instrumental work. It is not quite the same thing as "development" in the sense that this term was used by the classical symphonists: with them the theme did not *represent* anybody or anything—they regarded it as a musical phrase, pure and simple.

CHAPTER XVIII

THE LATER CLASSICAL PERIOD

O F the many eminent musicians who immediately succeeded Beethoven and profited by his example it is possible here to call attention to a few only in addition to those already referred to. Robert Schumann (1810-56), Felix Mendelssohn-Bartholdy (1809-47), and Johannes Brahms (1833-97) stand out especially (Wagner will be discussed in the next chapter). The fame of Schumann rests not only upon his compositions, but also upon his valuable work as a musical critic. Unlike many musicians, he was a man of considerable literary gifts. Although early in life he showed a decided talent for music, it was for a legal, not for a musical, career that he was trained. However, music and literature absorbed most of his attention, and he was particularly interested in the connection between these two arts. In 1834 he established a periodical *Die Neue Zeitschrift für Musik* ("The New Musical Times"), which soon became famous. He was not only a keen but a very generous critic, and helped to bring to performance many fine works both by old and contemporary masters which would otherwise have remained neglected.

Schumann's Works. As a composer, Schumann's reputation rests chiefly on his pianoforte works and songs, although he wrote some very fine chamber-music. Composers for the pianoforte still preferred to write their more serious music in Sonata Form; but as they gradually became more familiar with the possibilities and limitations of the instrument, they began to experiment in other musical forms. As we have seen, Chopin and Liszt were particularly successful; Schumann was even more enterprising. His best pianoforte compositions—*Papillons, Carnaval, Novelletten, Kreisleriana* and *Faschingswank aus Wien*—are really groups of pieces of varying length, and might almost be termed "Suites." As a rule, the themes are not developed in a continuous fashion, but each piece comprises a number of short contrasted sections repeated somewhat after the manner of a Rondo. Schumann discovered many novel effects obtainable from the pianoforte, particularly in regard to rhythm. His *Pianoforte Concerto* is probably the best loved of all compositions in that form.

Schumann's contributions to song-literature are of the highest importance. Schubert, who had no pretensions to any culture other than musical, seems occasionally to have read his poem superficially and then provided a musical setting without more ado. The result was successful if the poem had no meaning deeply hidden. But where Schubert sometimes failed, Schumann's literary training helped him to extract the last shade of meaning from the poem. Schumann's songs are not too well known in this country, probably for two reasons; first, the available translations of the German words are mostly ridiculous from a poetic point of view; secondly they demand more thought and more rehearsal than the average singer is prepared to give.

Mendelssohn. The case of Mendelssohn is somewhat peculiar. He was the idol of the musical public of his time, and it says much for his sterling character that he was not really spoilt. There never was a composer who from a social and financial point of view was so favoured by fortune as Mendelssohn. He was born in 1809, the same year as Chopin, and his father, a famous Hamburg banker, gave him every chance of developing his remarkable talent for music. Yet he was not altogether to be envied, for his charming personality together with his great ability and keenness for furthering the cause of music led to his being persuaded to undertake more work than his rather delicate constitution could stand, and he died of overwork at the early age of thirty-eight. In his lifetime, and for some years afterwards, he was regarded as second only to Beethoven, yet the number of his works regularly performed in the concert halls of to-day is exceedingly small, although he was quite a prolific composer. We shall attempt later to account for this. With the exception of Opera he essayed practically every branch of musical composition, and all of his works were eagerly sought after. One need not give a catalogue here, but only remark that amongst his works on a large scale only his oratorios *St Paul* and *Elijah,* together with the *Hymn of Praise,* really attract much attention to-day.

As an enthusiastic conductor and organiser Mendelssohn did splendid work. He arranged fine performances of the great classical works, and helped to create a wide interest in the works of Bach, which had been practically shelved for a hundred years. He gave in 1829 the first performance of Bach's *Matthew Passion*, which had for nearly a century been forgotten. *St. Paul* was largely based on Bach's work. This enterprise stimulated a revival of interest in Oratorio, which was none too flourishing at the time. But ten years later the production of *Elijah* marked an epoch in the history of that art-form. The story of Elijah is, of course, one of the strongest in dramatic interest; Mendelssohn seized on this feature and employed it so effectively that this oratorio has actually been staged, with some success, as a sacred opera.

Mendelssohn's music reflects the character of the man. He was extremely sensitive and anything rough or disagreeable caused him real distress. Consequently, even when the situation almost demanded harsh effects, as in the Baal choruses in *Elijah*, he shrinks from writing anything really ugly. This reticence is not appreciated in these days of realism. The influence of Mendelssohn over those who immediately succeeded him was not wholesome, especially in the sphere of choral music: he had too many imitators who, without his talent, tried to "go one better" and failed dismally. However, as an introduction to music of more vital interest Mendelssohn's works are excellent; e.g. his *Violin Concerto* is the most easily grasped of all works in that form, while his *Songs without Words* are charming examples of the short pianoforte piece.

Brahms. Brahms is the last of the great composers to adhere to the models established by the classical masters. He was concerned almost entirely with "absolute music"—music independent of any story or plot. The catalogue of his works contains such familiar terms as Sonata, Symphony, Concerto, String-Quartet, Variations, Songs, and so forth; Opera, however, is not included. He found these old forms elastic enough for the expression of his original ideas. He was never extravagant in his methods and had no desire to shock his audience. His music is mostly of a serious type; those who crave for excitement, violent contrasts, restlessness and freakishness find him dull. Brahms more than any other composer expects his audience to listen very intently all the time; directly one's attention begins to flag one gets bewildered. Like Browning, he is very concise, and not until the music has been repeatedly heard is it possible to grasp all that the composer has to say. By musicians who in the course of their work necessarily have to do with much music calling for little intelligence on their part, he is revered. Like Bach, he presents fascinating problems of interpretation, the solving of which keeps the imagination fresh. Details of considerable interest which at first were unsuspected reveal themselves after repeated performances and fall into their right places in the general scheme.

As a writer of songs, Brahms ranks with Schubert, Schumann and Hugo Wolf. These songs demand a

JOHANNES BRAHMS

cultured vocalist and pianist to do them anything like justice. The four Symphonies, of which probably the two first are the most easily grasped, are now included amongst the finest works of the type; while the *Variations* for orchestra, with the *Violin Concerto* and *Clarinet Quintet* [55] have already become highly appreciated. The *Requiem*, composed in 1868, is generally regarded not only as the finest choral work emanating from the period in which it was written, but as one of the masterpieces of musical imagination. His pianoforte music exhibits the characteristics mentioned above.

In adhering to our plan of dealing only with those composers whose works, as it were, "struck a new note," it will be necessary to refrain from mentioning a large number of musicians whose names frequently occur in catalogues of nineteenth century music.

Dvořák and Franck. The Bohemian, Dvořák, must, however, be mentioned. The catalogue of his works looks very much like that of any classical composer, and, in fact, he uses classical forms mostly. However, his genius for inventing striking and "catchy" melodies with piquant rhythm makes his music particularly easy to follow. His *"New World Symphony,"* which exhibits these characteristics, is his most popular orchestral work.

César Franck, a Belgian, who spent most of his life in Paris as an organist and music-teacher, was too

[55] At present not many gramophone reproductions of Brahms' music are available. But Records Nos. 26 and 110 are characteristic; also Col. L 1337 (Violin and Piano) and Col. L 1151 (String Quartet).

modest to gain much recognition in his lifetime. It would be difficult to name any other composer, now highly honoured, whose fame rests on such a few works. The best known are the *Symphony in D minor,* the *Sonata in A major* for Violin and Piano,[56] and the two works for Pianoforte: *Prélude, Choral et Fugue* and *Prélude, Aria et Finale.* Many consider that the two latter works are the finest compositions of any considerable length—not in Sonata Form—which have as yet been written for the pianoforte. Franck adopts a very expressive harmonic scheme, in which the possibilities of the older type of harmony are increased by a lavish use of chromatic notes and chords which sound peculiarly "modern."

[56] Records Nos. 29, 65.

Franck

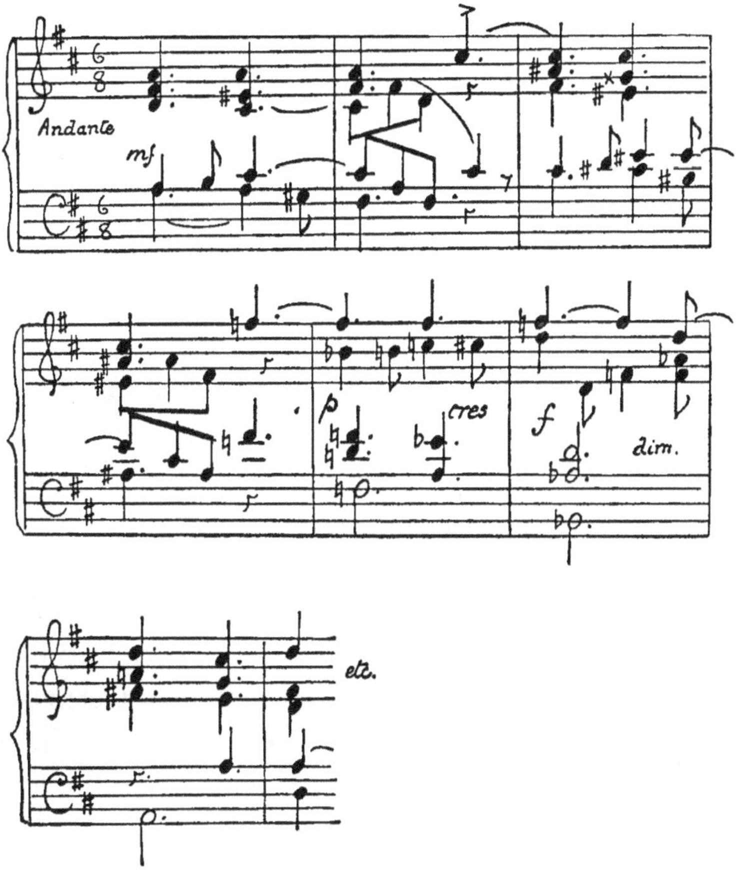

CHAPTER XIX

WAGNER

THE most outstanding musician of the second half of the nineteenth century was Richard Wagner. His career may be summarised thus. He was born at Leipzig in 1813 and received a liberal education, especially in literature, which stood him in good stead in later years. Unlike many great composers he did not produce anything of importance in his youth and early manhood; his first work of any note—the opera *Rienzi*—dates from 1842. This was followed by *The Flying Dutchman* in 1843. Meanwhile, he became much interested in legendary literature, of which Germany has a great store, and he came to the conclusion, which had also been reached by Weber, that these legends were better suited for operatic treatment than were the absurd stories upon which most Italian operas were based.

Struggle for Recognition. The most notable first-fruits of Wagner's deep study of mediæval legends appeared in the opera *Tannhäuser,* which was not at first a great success. However, Wagner was not the man to take criticism "lying down." Here his literary training was of advantage; by means of essays, pamphlets, speeches, and the production of poetical versions of the old legends, he insisted on being heard. He had on his side some of the most influential men of the day, including Liszt; and the musical public became sharply divided into Wagnerians and anti-Wagnerians. He was, besides, a violent politician, and before his next work *Lohengrin* could be produced he had to leave Germany in a hurry. During his exile he still carried on his literary campaign, making many enemies hereby. He spent much of his time in preparing for operatic treatment some of the legendary tales—throughout, Wagner wrote his own librettos. The old Celtic legend *Tristan und Isolde* especially appealed to him at this time, and an opera—or "Music Drama," as Wagner preferred to call it—founded on this legend was completed in 1859 and received its first performance at Munich in 1865.[57] This impassioned drama, which is as different from an Italian opera as it could well be, is considered by many to be Wagner's most original work. It is not surprising that Wagner had some trouble in securing a performance of *Tristan*. It makes such tremendous demands upon singers and instrumentalists alike that after fifty-seven rehearsals at Vienna it was put aside. Even *Tannhäuser,* a much simpler work, had to be rehearsed one hundred and sixty-four times before it could be presented to the Parisian public.

In 1862 Wagner was allowed to return to Germany, and in 1863 he produced a poetical version of an ancient legend "The Ring of the Nibelungs" *(Der*

---

[57] There are many Records of Wagner's works available. See Appendix IV.

Ring des Nibelungen). He intended to use this as the libretto of a lengthy Music Drama divided into four sections: *Das Rheingold, Die Walküre, Siegfried,* and *Götterdämmerung.* Wagner did not expect to live long enough to complete the music, and published the poem as "a literary product." A copy fell into the hands of Ludwig II, King of Bavaria, a most extraordinary and fantastic monarch with more than a taint of insanity. He took an intense delight in all forms of art, especially music, and he invited Wagner to settle in Bavaria and proceed with his work. Freed for a time from his anxiety about money-matters he proceeded with the music of *Der Ring.* Partly as a relief from the strain of composing such a huge work, he laid this aside for a time and wrote a comic opera *Die Meistersinger,* which is really a "Tournament of Song." This is probably the finest opera ever written by Wagner or anybody else, and on its production in 1868 it was enthusiastically received.

His success. Although by this time Wagner had become the most prominent—if not the best-loved—of living composers, the hindrances in the way of getting a performance of the whole of *Der Ring* seemed unsurmountable. No theatre well enough equipped for the production of such a colossal work existed; and in any event the cost would be enormous. But interest in Wagner had been roused to such an extent that a method of overcoming the difficulties was found by his influential friends. A subscription list was opened in several countries, and the response was good enough to warrant the erection of an entirely new opera-house at the little town of Bayreuth, in which no expense was to be spared in giving performances of *Der Ring* under the best possible conditions. This scheme was carried through successfully, and in 1876 the whole of *Der Ring* was performed, making a great sensation. Thenceforward, the Wagner Festivals, at which all the important Wagnerian Music Dramas were produced, became an important feature of musical life. Wagner's last work was *Parsifal,* a semireligious drama founded on legends connected with the Holy Grail.

Wagner's principles. Let us very briefly try to summarise the principles upon which Wagner founded his Music Dramas; he himself has told us what they are. Firstly, he thought that Opera had not reached the point of excellence to which it could attain. In the typical Italian opera nearly everything was subordinated to the music; the actual literary value of the libretto was hardly taken into account. So long as this provided opportunities for the introduction of Arias and concerted music, well and good. The operatic public of the day went to hear fine *singing;* if the acting was passable, the plot not altogether too stupid, the stage-setting attractive, and the instrumental accompaniment not too uninteresting, all the better. Of course, as Mozart and others proved, it is quite possible to write a good opera on these lines. But with Wagner the dramatic element was of paramount importance. However fine a song might be from a musical standpoint, if it does not exactly fit in with the situation it ought not to be introduced. If the drama does not actually demand a series of choruses, then they ought to be dispensed with. (In the whole of *Tristan* there are only a few bars of choral music.) Again, the acting and stage-setting must receive as much attention as the music. From a dramatic standpoint, it is absurd to sing prose to a formal song-tune; therefore this should be reserved for the purely lyrical sections. We shall see below how Wagner tackled this problem.

Extension of Vocabulary. Once more, he found that in order to secure an adequate representation of his ideas an extension of the current musical vocabulary was necessary, especially in connection with harmony. Of course, Wagner's predecessors knew perfectly well that an enormous number of chords can be built up out of the ninety or so musical sounds which can be produced on musical instruments. But, as we have already seen, the earlier composers considered that only a few of the possible number of note-combinations were smooth enough for use. As time went on, and composers felt it necessary to extend their vocabulary, they admitted chords of a slight degree of harshness, provided that this harshness was modified by placing such chords in a particular context, i.e. "resolving" them. It is a somewhat remarkable fact that the human ear will soon tolerate chords which at first seem hopelessly ugly. Hence we find that succeeding generations of composers added new combinations to the chordal stock-in-trade, and found new and varied methods of resolving discords. But the classical composers drew a definite line between combinations which, whether pleasant or not, were at least capable of being regarded as music, and those which were thought too hideous for use except in the rarest of circumstances. However, Wagner declined to be bound in this matter; he did not scruple to use any chords whatever if they suited his purpose. But, as a rule, even his most weird progressions of chords are built up on the simplest harmonic foundations; the discords are usually the result of using "ornamental" notes very freely. E.g.

From *Tristan*

is only an ornamented version of:

Moreover, Wagner makes very extensive use of the expressive power of "Modulation," i.e. a change of key-centre; this can be well seen in the opening phrases of the "Liebestod" in *Tristan*.

Prominence given to Orchestra. It has been said already that in the classical operas the "prose" sections of the libretto were usually set to a bald type of Recitative in free time. Intermediate between that and the Aria another musical form called "Arioso" was used by some composers, in which the vocal part was something like Recitative, but more regular, so as to permit of an accompaniment in strict time. This accompaniment was generally founded on a little phrase continually repeated more or less exactly. (Nearly all of the Arias in Bach's *Matthew Passion* are preceded by an Arioso.) After all, it is only occasionally in a drama that a formal song is called for, or that the verbal phrases are so "prosy" that the plainest style of Recitative is demanded. To get over the difficulty Wagner adopted a style which is something like that of the Arioso, only much more elaborate. The orchestral part is not now merely a little figure of accompaniment but a tissue of "leading themes" (see p. 150) varied in many ways and interwoven in contrapuntal fashion. Hence, the chief interest generally lies in the orchestral part; in fact, this was often written first. It is so complete in itself that with a very little editing it is possible to play long extracts from the Music Dramas in the concert-room with the vocal part omitted. From one point of view a Wagnerian Music Drama is a long Symphonic Poem for voices and orchestra combined with stage-action. The plan of sharing the interest between voices and orchestra, instead of using the latter merely to *accompany* the singers, is now well-established, and has, moreover, played a great part in the development not only of solo-song but of the short dramatic Cantata which has almost superseded the Oratorio in public favour.

The advance in the art of orchestration made by Wagner cannot be demonstrated without a long series of extracts. It must suffice to state that he demands a very large orchestra, not for the sake of making more noise, but in order to obtain more variety of tone-colour. E.g. by adding an alto oboe (cor anglais) and double-bassoon to the two oboes and two bassoons generally employed, he is able to obtain six-part harmony from the double-reed instruments. The Bayreuth orchestra numbered no fewer than 114 players.

It is now a comparatively easy matter for the student to make practical acquaintance with Wagner's methods. Short of hearing the works performed as written, he can obtain excellent arrangements in varied forms. From a consideration of the principles adopted, it is clear that one ought to become thoroughly acquainted with the "leading themes" and their individual significance, and this can be satisfactorily secured if the student takes one or other of the "Guides" to the Wagnerian Music Dramas and studies it either in conjunction with a pianoforte-duet arrangement or with the gramophone records. The duet arrangements are usually devoid of technical difficulty, but in using the records with the vocal score the listener must be prepared for big "cuts." Perhaps the most fruitful way of beginning the study of Wagner is to become familiar with the *Siegfried Idyll*, an entrancing Serenade founded on themes from the *Ring*.[58]

Other Operatic Composers. Several types of opera can be distinguished besides "Grand Opera," in which all the words are sung. There is the German "Singspiel," of which Mozart's *Magic Flute* and Beethoven's *Fidelio* are good examples: here the dialogue is spoken, not sung. In France this variety of opera is called "Opéra comique"; not that the subject-matter need be comic—a humorous opera of this type is usually styled "Opéra bouffe." Offenbach was a specialist in this form, but nothing better has been done on these lines than the series of Gilbert and Sullivan operas. The early operas of Verdi, of which *Aïda*[59] is a good specimen, were frankly Italian operas of the usual type, but in his two latest operas, *Otello*[60] and *Falstaff*, he adopted Wagner's plan of making the music more continuous and of assigning a more important role to the orchestra. The younger Italian composers, e.g. Puccini and Léoncavallo, adopt the same plan. The most noted German operatic composer of to-day—Richard Strauss—is frankly Wagnerian, and in the dramas *Salome*[61] and *Elektra* he does not shrink from accentuating by means of his music the brutality and horror which is presented in these tragedies.

[58] Record No. 106.

[59] The complete opera has been recorded by Col.

[60] Record No. 78.

[61] Record No. 79.

Russian opera will be referred to in the next chapter. Meanwhile, one must not omit to call attention to Debussy's *Pelléas et Mélisande*. Here music is used chiefly to create an "atmosphere," or a "background" to the drama itself. There are no tunes in the ordinary sense of the term, and apart from the drama the music would be meaningless. The vocal part is something like a Gregorian Chant, and this, combined with the peculiar harmonisation which is characteristic of Debussy, gives a kind of "unearthly" effect which for many listeners has a strong fascination. This opera, together with Dargomyisky's *Stone Guest*—its forerunner, stands in a class by itself.

Although Opera enshrines some of the finest music ever written, this form of art makes but a limited appeal to the English public; at any rate, Englishmen do not wax sufficiently enthusiastic about it to provide the funds necessary to meet the heavy expenses which would be entailed in the presentation of Opera on an extensive scale. It may be that the average Englishman is repelled by the artificiality which is inseparable from Grand Opera, but really good examples of "Opéra comique" like the Gilbert and Sullivan operas[62] are always welcomed.

While the immense importance of Wagner's contributions to dramatic music must be fully recognised, it is not necessary to assume that the older form of Opera, usually termed "Italian," is entirely out-of-date. The latter is constructed on a different plan from that adopted by Wagner, and it is a matter of opinion as to

[62] Some of these are recorded complete by H.M.V.

which is the best. While we may be lost in admiration of *Tristan,* it is not necessary to pretend that it is on a higher artistic level than Mozart's *Magic Flute* or Verdi's *Rigoletto;* and it is safe to say that the better Italian operas, ancient and modern, will not for a long time lose their charm for all sincere lovers of art.

CHAPTER XX

MUSIC AND NATIONALITY

IT will doubtless have been noticed that in the last few chapters we have been concerned entirely with the music of Germany, Italy and France. It is true that musicians of other nationalities were prominent in the nineteenth century, but in the main they adopted the forms and phraseology which were current in the three countries named. As we have seen in the case of Weber, the idea of Nationalism had been gaining ground; German music for Germans, French music for Frenchmen was demanded, and even British music for Britons has lately come to be advocated. Let us see, however, what is actually possible in this direction. One may, for instance, take Folk-tunes belonging to a particular nationality and arrange these in various ways, as Grieg has done with Norwegian tunes. (His harmonisation, however, is anything but "Norwegian.") Also it is possible to use Folk-melodies as the main themes of a Symphony or Symphonic Poem which, in other respects, is of the usual type. Also one may write songs in the style of the Folk-songs of a particular nation. Clearly this will not lead us very far. Most of the musical material used by composers of all nationalities is common property. It would be meaningless to talk about *German* Harmony, the *French* Orchestra,

British Melody, and so forth. Moreover, the human voice, regarded as a musical instrument, does not vary according to nationality. But there is another possibility. A composer who knows thoroughly the Folk-music of his native country may seek to preserve in his works the *spirit* of that music, without actually quoting it. E.g. the main feature of English Folk-music is directness, simplicity, and most often cheery optimism; that of Hungary is strongly rhythmic; that of Italy is very melodious with hardly a trace of that pathos which is so evident in Irish Folk-music. These features can, of course, be incorporated in original music.

Russian Music. Towards the end of the nineteenth century, the musical public of Western Europe rather suddenly became alive to the fact that there had been for some decades important musical happenings in Russia. The first Russian composer to gain a reputation outside his own country was Tschaikowsky.[63] But there is little distinctively Russian about his music (Mozart was his idol), except that he sometimes uses the Folk-tunes of his native country instead of inventing original themes and that his larger works are "full-blooded" in character—sometimes savage, sometimes over-sentimental, and often despondent; in such respects they reflect Russian life. It has been well said that when Tschaikowsky wants to portray any emotion he "lays it on with a trowel." But his Symphonies, which are of a classical pattern, are easy to listen to, full of melody and splendidly laid out for the orchestra. They do not, however, seem to "wear well."

[63] See Records Nos. 28, 41, 52.

Opera, perhaps, forms the best field for the display of Nationalism in music. In 1836 Glinka produced an opera, *Life for the Tsar;* he declared that in this work his countrymen would "feel at home." It was received enthusiastically, and a little band of talented composers, Balakiref, Cui, Borodin, Moussorgsky and Rimsky-Korsakoff, went further in this direction. Their operas are mostly founded on events in Russian history or on Russian folk-lore, and the music faithfully reflects the barbaric splendour,tragedy and passion associated with "Holy Russia." The operas best known outside Russia are *Prince Igor,*[64] *Khovanshchina,* and *Boris Godounof.*[65] In the latter Folk-tunes are freely used.

An important feature in Russian musical life is the "Ballet," for which in the time of the Tsars lavish provision was made. The Russian Ballet comprises something else than superb dancing; it often partakes of the nature of an opera without words or of a Symphonic Poem with stage-movements. This obviously affords much scope for an enterprising composer. Amongst others, Rimsky-Korsakoff wrote some remarkable ballet music,[66] which bears transference to the concert-room. Stravinski's ballets *Petroushka, The Fire Bird,*[67] and *The Rite of Spring* are typical of ultra-modern music, which will be considered in the next chapter.

[64] Record No. 89.

[65] Records Nos. 87, 88.

[66] Record No. 53.

[67] Record No. 59.

CHAPTER XXI

LATER DEVELOPMENTS

IN this concluding chapter it is proposed to deal briefly with what is sometimes called "ultra-modern music."[68] A goodly number of musicians of the present day find that the musical vocabulary and musical forms which have been slowly evolved through the labours of the classical composers and extended by Wagner and his immediate successors are comprehensive enough for the presentation of their ideas. Such composers as Parry, Stanford, Elgar,[69] Delius, Glazounoff and Vincent d'Indy may be named in this connection. Others, again, say that it is impossible to write any more music which is really original, unless it is permitted to use all available musical material in entirely new ways and to add to the existing musical vocabulary a considerable amount of material which has hitherto been excluded. These revolutionaries do not agree that the description of music as "a concourse of sweet sounds" is comprehensive enough. They say, rightly or wrongly, that "sweetness" and "beauty," in the sense in which most people understand these terms, represent

[68] The following Records well exhibit the chief characteristics of this school of composers: Nos. 50, 57, 58, 59, 60, 70, 114.

[69] See Records Nos. 33, 37, 128.

only one aspect of the art. It must be allowed that much of this "new" music is not so original as it pretends to be. It depends for its novel effect largely upon tricks which have been known for centuries, but which older composers have declined to use except for very special purposes.

New Scales. Clearly, this ultra-modern music must be regarded as experimental; much of it will soon be forgotten and some time must elapse before the value of any particular experiment can be determined. Meanwhile let us see in what directions experimental work can be carried on. First, classical composers, and those who follow their methods, use for melodic purposes the scales known as major and minor almost exclusively. But there is no reason why other scales, of which a large number are available (see p. 25), should not be used, and some writers—Busoni for instance—have experimented with many such scales. Debussy,[70] Ravel,[71] and other French composers often adopt the whole-tone scale—C, D, E, F sharp, G sharp, A sharp, C. Since the interval between any two adjacent notes of this series is always one tone, the variety afforded in the major and minor scales by the admixture of tones and semitones is wanting here. Another feature of the whole-tone scale is that all the chords derived therefrom are alike in quality, e.g. G♯ A♯ etc., since they all
    E F♯
    C D
consist of two major thirds superimposed. The poverty

[70] See Records Nos. 28, 56, 61, 111.

[71] Record No. 113.

of this scale is soon apparent when the novelty has
worn off.

Saint-Saëns

Then there is the twelve-note scale, which is the
familiar chromatic scale, but all the notes are regarded
as of equal importance; there is no key-note and consequently no idea of tonality. A cat walking over the
pianoforte keyboard will produce an effect of this
kind. The experiment does not sound promising, but
Scriabin has written some pieces in the twelve-note
scale which are not at all hideous. Nevertheless, music
based on this principle can never sound to us other than
strange, because it clashes with our ingrained sense
of tonality, which is here altogether contradicted (see
example below). Another grave disadvantage is that by
adopting the twelve-note scale one cannot make use of
the expressive power of modulation, i.e. change of key,
for here there is no "key" at all. The wonderful effect
of modulation can well be studied in the middle and
final sections of the second movement of Schubert's
Unfinished Symphony.

Modern Rhythm. Secondly, while the resources of melody, especially vocal melody, are in danger of being exhausted, the same need not be said of Rhythm. Considering the immense number of possible rhythms, it seems strange that the classical composers should have restricted themselves to the use of only a few varieties. In rhythmic sensibility they were far behind the ancient Greeks. They seldom used any other times but duple, triple and quadruple, whereas quintuple and septuple times are quite intelligible. Schumann and Brahms, especially, endeavoured by means of syncopation and such devices to impart more variety into Rhythm. Modern writers are fond of alternating one kind of time with another, e.g.

The complicated rhythms of "jazz" are quite legitimate results of an attempt to obtain rhythmic variety.

New Chords. Again, if one is prepared to agree that *any* possible combination of notes can be regarded as a chord, and as such ought to be admitted into our musical system, then we have by no means come to the end of our harmonic resources. There are dozens of ways of harmonising a simple tune, so that if it is almost impossible nowadays to invent an original melody, it is easy, by the use of unusual harmony, to disguise its familiar features. This procedure is frequently adopted in modern songs. There are certain limits to the capacity of a singer to sing difficult intervals, but the accompanist is not hampered in this way. The basic chord of the classical composer was "the common chord"; and, as a rule his themes were projected against a background of common chords and the simplest of discords. E.g. the main theme of Beethoven's *Eroica* Symphony is obviously founded on the common chord E flat, G and B flat.

Now, suppose one uses, as Scriabin does, this combination as the basic chord:

clearly we shall have a new harmonic basis, and melody founded thereon will sound novel.

Once more, the modern composer does not feel compelled to "round off" his discords by "resolving" them; in fact all modern writers—not only the ultra-moderns—avail themselves of this liberty, but only the latter are bold enough to write strings of discords which seem to have little connection of any kind between them.

Cyril Scott

One must not think of harmony as a series of isolated chords; the effect of any chord depends largely upon its context. E.g. the chord $\begin{matrix} A\flat \\ F \\ D\flat \end{matrix}$ has quite a different effect when it occurs between two chords definitely in key C from its effect when placed between chords founded upon the scale of D flat.

Another device largely used by "advanced" writers is to raise or depress by a semitone one or more of the notes of a familiar chord. Thus the chord $\begin{matrix} G \\ E \\ C \end{matrix}$ may be altered thus: $\begin{matrix} G \\ E \\ C\sharp \end{matrix}$ $\begin{matrix} G \\ E \\ C\flat \end{matrix}$ $\begin{matrix} G \\ E\sharp \\ C \end{matrix}$ $\begin{matrix} G\flat \\ E \\ C \end{matrix}$ $\begin{matrix} G\flat \\ E\flat \\ C \end{matrix}$ and so on.

Discords also may be altered in this fashion, producing strange results.

Also a note or notes may be added to chords to which these added notes do not normally belong. E.g. into the last chord $\begin{smallmatrix}G\\E\\C\end{smallmatrix}$ of a cadence in key C such a

note as A may be added $\begin{smallmatrix}C\\A\\G\\E\\C\end{smallmatrix}$. Debussy is very partial

to this effect, as may be seen in the *Children's Corner*. Observe that this procedure may result in the formation of chords containing many notes, e.g.

In the above example by Ravel, the added notes are A and E in the first chord and D in the second. (Cf. in this connection the ancient device called the "Pedal." See p. 47.)

In most of these complicated chords it will inevitably happen that two notes a semitone apart are sounded together; this makes the strongest of all possible clashes. It is necessary to remember, however, that the discordant effect of such combinations depends upon several factors, and it is imperative to play them with precisely that degree of loudness or softness indicated by the composer. A combination which sounds ugly when played *f* or *mf* in the middle of the pianoforte keyboard may be quite tolerable when played *pp* in an upper octave, while even a common chord sounds harsh when played in the lower octaves. Again, some chordal progressions designed to be played by stringed instruments may be quite smooth under those conditions, but intolerably ugly when played on the pianoforte.

The chordal system with which we are all familiar is built up on a series of superimposed thirds, thus:

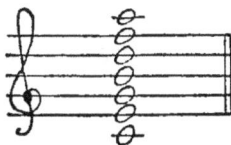

but that is no reason why one should not experiment with a chordal system built up on fourths, thus:

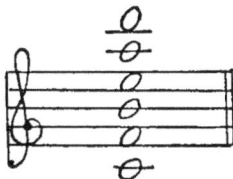

This will, of course, produce new harmonic effects. Schönberg and Cyril Scott (cf. his second *Poème*) have experimented in this direction.

Extension of Counterpoint. Modern Counterpoint makes considerable demands upon the listeners. Most people find it difficult enough to follow two melodies proceeding simultaneously, as often happens in a Fugue. But now we are asked to disentangle passages in which, perhaps, the stringed instruments are playing a certain progression of chords in one key while the wind instruments have another progression in quite a different key. Obviously these two progressions will not "fit" at all in the ordinary sense. Take a simple example. There is no mechanical difficulty in playing "Three Blind Mice" on one pianoforte in key D while a second player plays "Golden Slumbers" in the key of A flat. If we attempt to listen to the *combination* of these two tunes—in other words, try to make them "fit"—the result is hideous; but is it possible to hear them as separate tunes? The answer is "Yes," if one is prepared to spend a considerable time in practising this operation. The real trouble is that it is hard to break the habit acquired very early in life of amalgamating perceptions which occur simultaneously. In some cases there is no difficulty; e.g. the notes of the bells in Tschaikowsky's 1812 *Overture*[72] only rarely fit into the harmony played by the orchestra; but, because the "quality" of the bell-tones is so different from that of all the orchestral instruments, we do not attempt to combine them, and hear the passage as two separate streams of sound. This process is usually referred to as "listening horizontally." Only on the assumption that one can listen in this fashion is it possible to make head

[72] Record No. K-05046 (Voc.).

or tail of many passages met with in modern works.[73]

Increase of Orchestra. The composers of recent Ballet-music, especially Stravinski, have tried to obtain novel orchestral effects by using the instruments in unusual combinations. This applies particularly to instruments of percussion: drums, cymbals, gongs, etc. They have also introduced instruments from which no musical tone—only a noise—can be extracted. There is nothing new about the combination of noise with musical tone; a note on the violin is partly noise (the scrape of the bow), and it is only too well known that a note played on the pianoforte is partly "thud." But speaking generally, no really new musical instruments of importance have lately been invented, though great advances have been made in the construction of wind-instruments, especially in connection with the brass. It is now possible to play passages on horns and trumpets which would be quite impracticable for instruments of that type made, say, fifty years ago.[74] In fact, the military band, which until quite recently was restricted to playing music of little artistic value, promises to become a serious rival to the orchestra.

Modern Forms. It remains only to refer to Musical Form as exemplified in recent compositions. After all, the number of musical forms which are shapely enough to be used with effect is not great, and most modern writers still find that the familiar forms, Opera, Sonata,

---

[73] Those who wish to pursue this subject further should consult *Modern Harmony* by Hull (Augener) or *Modern Harmony* by Lenormand (Joseph Williams).

[74] See Appendix i.

Symphony, Suite, Variations, Concerto, Dramatic Cantata, and so forth, are adequate. Perhaps the most noteworthy feature in modern works is the tendency to use the shorter forms—the Prelude, Overture, Phantasy, Nocturne, etc. In spite of the use of a large variety of such titles it will generally be found that a work can be described as an example of one of the older forms more or less modified.

Many of the most talented composers of to-day— e.g. Delius, Vaughan-Williams, Holst and Bax—do not adopt the newer methods exclusively, but introduce into the texture of their music only some of those features cherished by the extremists. Anything like a complete list of composers of the ultra-modern school would be of no value; it would have to be continually revised; and no one can yet say which of the novelties of to-day will prove to be only a nine-days' wonder, and which will retain a permanent place in musical literature. The great difficulty which the modernists have to face lies in the fact that the minds of the listeners are already stored with musical memories based on the older system; however hard they try, listeners cannot help *comparing*. Take a simple instance. Play "Three Blind Mice" in D major, but play all the G's as G sharps. One gets a nasty shock now and then. Why is this? Firstly, because these G sharps clash with the G's which our memory leads us to expect; secondly, the G sharps throw the tune into a Mode (v) which is comparatively unfamiliar. Unless the composer is careful, the impression he conveys will not be that he is writing original harmony, but that he is writing old-fashioned harmony with a number of *mistakes* in it.

Themes in Modern Music. Another difficulty which confronts the listener is this: until comparatively recently, writers of instrumental music in the symphonic style were very careful to make their most important themes stand out so prominently that no one was left in doubt as to which were these main themes. In order to secure this prominence, composers deliberately made the rest of the music less strikingly melodic. In the form of a diagram their procedure in this respect may roughly be shown thus:

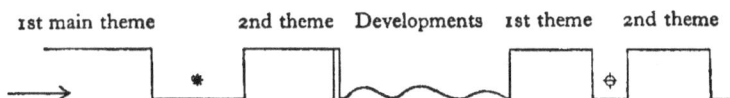

The sections ✳ and ⊕ were usually of subordinate interest, although the more eminent composers, e.g. Beethoven, took care that they should not give the impression of mere "padding." Modern writers, in their anxiety to avoid this defect, frequently introduce here subordinate themes of considerable interest, but this device, of course, detracts somewhat from the

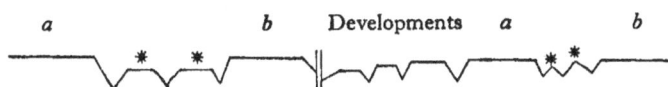

prominence normally given to the main themes. Thus:

Here *a* and *b* represent the main themes and ✳ denotes subordinate themes.

Again, the main themes themselves in modern works are often not tunes in the ordinary sense, but are short passages founded upon a striking rhythmic figure or series of chords. Here are two of the main themes from Strauss' *Tod und Verklärung*.

The first and last movements of Elgar's *Second Symphony* well exhibit the procedure shown above. Obviously, the listener must not expect to appreciate such a work until it has been heard several times.

It is too soon to say whether the attempts of certain modern composers to extend the scope of the Symphonic Poem so as to make it a vehicle for expounding philosophic systems will come to anything. Richard Strauss has taken the philosophy of Nietzsche as the basis of his tone-poem *Also sprach Zarathustra,* and Scriabin in his *Poem of Fire* tries to expound musically the ideas underlying Theosophy.

New Choral Music. Modern developments in instrumental music have been responsible for a great change in the style of accompanied Choral Music. In the older type most stress was laid on the vocal side; the orchestra, when not playing independently, was regarded rather as a support for the voices; at any rate, choir and orchestra were mutually dependent. Moreover, the choir was rarely asked to sing anything which absolutely demanded instrumental support. Any melodic interval can, of course, be played; but some intervals are very difficult to sing in tune, and composers recognised such limitations. This can be seen in the case of the old Madrigals and in any of the sacred or secular Cantatas of the early nineteenth century, or even later. But composers in these days introduce into the vocal part without compunction intervals, rhythms and chords which, without the addition of an orchestra, would be impracticable and meaningless. Further still, they take advantage, even in unaccompanied music, of the advance made by choirs in technical skill, so that such a work as Holst's *Hymn of Jesus,* built up by the lavish use of all the resources of modern harmony, rhythm, and instrumentation, seems to have almost nothing in common with music of the Mendelssohnian type. In short, in modern choral works of any pretensions the choir is treated rather as a "human orchestra"; whereas in the earliest stages of instrumental music the instrumental parts were founded on *vocal* melody and harmony.

Summary. We have now come to the end of our survey of the growth of music. It may be well very briefly to sum up. It has been seen that of the materials—rhythm, melody and harmony—out of which music is made,

189

rhythm appeared first, then melody in a very crude form, and then after an interval measured by thousands of years came the development of harmony. Leaving Folk-music out of account, music as an organised form of Art, and in the sense in which the term is used to-day, is of comparatively recent growth. Not until well on in the sixteenth century A.D. do we find any considerable mass of music which appeals to us now as much more than experimental, although it is possible to find isolated examples of real artistic value. Music, like philosophy, was for hundreds of years under the fostering care of the Church, so that it was Church music which at first received almost a monopoly of attention. Instrumental music, except for the organ, was for long regarded as of less importance than pure vocal music; the latter in the form of unaccompanied choral music being brought to a high state of perfection in the sixteenth century. This period also saw the high development of a particular kind of secular vocal music, viz. the "Madrigal." Then came the establishment of the new forms of Opera and Oratorio, which progressed very rapidly. Opera soon demanded that increased attention should be given to instruments and instrumental music, so that this form of the art soon began to assume independent importance, not only as regards individual instruments, but also in connection with these grouped to form a band, big or little.

From this time onwards, the development of music may be compared with that of a rapidly-growing tree, continually throwing off fresh branches, these being represented by much modified or quite new forms:

Fugue, Suite, Sonata, Cantata, Chamber-music, Art Song, Symphonic Poem, and so forth, these forms becoming gradually more distinct from one another.

With Bach and others in the eighteenth century we find that they were in possession of a musical vocabulary extensive enough to enable them to use it more and more confidently as a means for the expression of profound ideas. The problem of finding a satisfactory framework for building thereon a long work for instruments only was solved for the time being by Haydn, and his principles were adopted not only by Mozart and Beethoven, but by a host of composers of less eminence. Then came the development of the "Art Song" by Schubert, Schumann, Brahms, and others, and a tendency to introduce the spirit of Romanticism into instrumental music in particular. The great improvement in the construction of the pianoforte led to this instrument assuming great prominence in musical life. The illustrative possibilities of music were exploited by Berlioz, Liszt and many others; this has led to the popularity of the musical form known as the "Tone-" or "Symphonic Poem."

Wagner's revolutionary ideas on the subject of Music Drama monopolised most of the attention of the musical world during the middle of the nineteenth century, and his triumph before the end of the century was complete. His new contributions to musical vocabulary in connection with harmony, especially, were eagerly appropriated by others, and have influenced all branches of music ever since. The nineteenth century also saw the rapid rise of a group of Russian composers, who brought into music some emotional elements which had seldom before been included. In the last two decades of this century a strong desire manifested itself on the part of young composers to experiment in ways already described, and such experiments are still proceeding. It must, however, be granted that the great classical works are as popular as ever.

The Interpreter. It is inevitable that in a short treatise like this little attention can be bestowed on those who come between a composer and his audience. Possibly it is a disadvantage to music that there has to be a kind of "middle-man"—an interpreter or performer, in fact.[75] This is not the case with Painting, Sculpture, and most other arts. Clearly, the composer and his music are quite at the mercy of the middle-man; many a fine work has been ruined by a bad performance, while too often a poor work gains popularity—short-lived, possibly—through an excellent performance. It is therefore only a want of space which can excuse the absence of mention of many names of performers who by their efforts have helped the cause of music. Moreover, there is the difficulty that we simply do not and cannot know the standard of excellence reached by performers now no longer with us. Written records are of little value; what was adjudged excellent in the eighteenth century might now be considered only good. But there is every reason to believe that those artists such as Liszt and Jenny Lind who were recognised as giants in their day must have been little, if at all, inferior to their successors;

[75] We can ignore the rare instances in which the composer, by himself, performs his own works.

otherwise composers would not have written as they did. It is, however, certain that there are at the present day many more first-rate performers, both amateur and professional, than ever before, while audiences are much larger and generally more critical. The slipshod methods of many of the older writers of Symphonies and such-like serious works would be laughed at to-day.

The Conductor and Critic. Once again, the orchestral conductor is a much more important personage than he used to be. The individual player in a large modern orchestra has no notion of the effect of his playing; e.g. if he is a viola player and the bass-trombonist sits just behind him, he probably hears hardly at all the sounds he himself is producing! "Expression marks" are usually of vague meaning and may be altogether misleading. The player has to rely mostly upon the conductor, who thereby assumes a tremendous responsibility. The latter has to regard himself as the real interpreter of the music; the band is an instrument upon which he plays. Curiously enough, in England at any rate, the conductor—as the term is now understood—is a modern institution; he used to sit at the pianoforte and occasionally beat time, but his influence over the orchestra was very limited. It was the "leader" of the band who kept, or tried to keep, the band together by vigorous flourishes of his bow. But Mendelssohn on his visits to England introduced the continental practice of giving the conductor undivided control. The first great *virtuoso* conductor was Hans von Bülow (*b.* 1830), who helped materially in the production of Wagner's works, while amongst other great orchestral conductors ought to be named Hans Richter, Arthur Nikisch, Felix Weingartner, Sir Henry Wood and Albert Coates.

The influence of the great critics and writers on musical subjects has been of much importance. The business of the critics is by virtue of their long experience to call attention to really good music which might otherwise be overlooked, and to point out deficiencies which at first can only be detected by one who is in constant touch with artistic affairs. The first really great musical critic of modern times was Schumann. Sir George Grove, Joseph Bennett, Sir Hubert Parry and Ernest Newman have done critical work of the first order in England.

The Future. In an old magazine of 1871 the writer asserts as an astonishing fact that he knew of "a London schoolmaster who eighteen years ago succeeded in teaching a class of about thirty boys actually to sing from notes!" The novelty of 1853 has become a commonplace of 1923, and it is significant of the enormous strides made in the musical education of the country at large, thanks to the efforts of teachers like Hullah, Curwen, Somervell, and Stewart Macpherson. But probably it is the advent of the gramophone and wireless which will be noted by the future historian as the beginning of a new era in music, and these inventions are only in the initial stages of development. Listeners to all kinds of music are now to be numbered by the hundred thousand instead of by hundreds. What effect this may ultimately have cannot yet be even guessed. What would Beethoven have said could he have known that on one particular evening in 1923 his *Seventh Symphony* would be heard by something like half-a-million people at once! A somewhat curious fact in connection with wireless is that one realises that the effect of a performance depends to some extent on what one *sees* as well as hears. The stimulating influence of being one of a large audience is wanting; the music has to stand or fall on its own merits, and it is remarkable how strongly the "bad patches" in the music are revealed. All "listeners-in" are receiving ear-training of an intensive type, even if this be informal, and the most intelligent of them are fast becoming critical. Also, for them, musical history takes on a new meaning. The late Sir John Stainer used to say that at any moment some new discovery in the world of sound might well revolutionise the whole position of musical art. Perhaps that moment has already arrived.

THE MODERN ORCHESTRA

THE orchestra of to-day comprises three groups of instruments: strings, wind, and percussion. The principles underlying tone-production in stringed instruments have been already explained (see p. 3). The instruments of this class used in the modern orchestra are the violin, viola, violoncello, and double-bass. The lowest note obtainable with the usual tuning on each instrument is as shown:

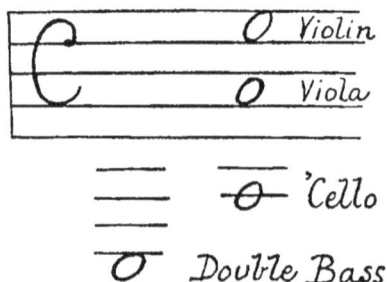

The upper limit on all of these instruments is not fixed, but beyond a certain range the tone is thin and difficult to control.

The harp is sometimes found in the orchestra, but its features are too familiar to require explanation. The

mechanism of the wind instruments, however, is not
well known.

There are two groups of wind instruments: the
brass and the woodwind. If we take an open pipe or
tube, either straight, curved, or coiled, 8 feet in length,
and by some means cause the column of air inside it
to vibrate as a whole, we shall obtain a low note, C,
identical with the lowest note of a 'cello. This is called the
"fundamental" note of the tube. But it is also possible to
make this column of air vibrate in two halves; it is then
found that the note produced is one octave higher than
the fundamental: this note is called the "first harmonic."
Also it is possible to make the air-column vibrate in
thirds, quarters, fifths, etc., giving the third, fourth, fifth,
etc. harmonics. So that, from the one 8 ft. tube these
sounds theoretically can be obtained:

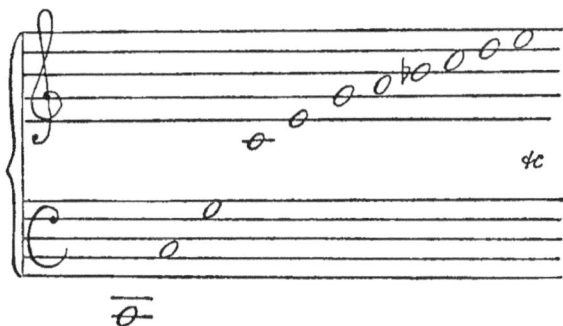

(The B flat is slightly "out of tune.")

We may therefore regard our tube as a wind instrument with an incomplete scale. But, as a matter of fact,
there are other practical difficulties connected with
such an instrument. On any particular instrument, if

the fundamental is easy to produce (it seldom is), then the upper harmonics will not come easily, and vice versa. Thus only a few harmonics are actually possible on one instrument; if we want other notes we shall have to use an instrument with a different fundamental. The army bugle is a tube whose fundamental is C (second space, bass stave). This note is difficult to get, but the first five harmonics can be obtained with reasonable facility:

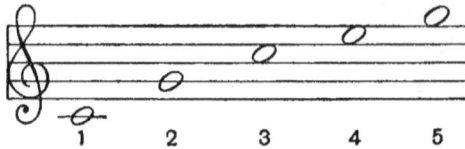

All the army bugle calls are confined to these five notes. But methods of getting over this difficulty have been devised, all depending on the fact that if the "speaking" length of the tube is extended or shortened, then the pitch of the note or notes is correspondingly lowered or raised. E.g. a player manipulating the 8 ft. instrument mentioned above can add extra pieces of tubing ("crooks"), and the whole series of notes will then be lowered by a certain interval, dependent upon the length of this added tubing. Suppose, for instance, that a composition is in the key of B major. The player on an 8 ft. instrument, using only the "natural" notes, would have a very slack time; he could normally produce only one note of the scale, viz. E, but by adding a crook of appropriate length he could depress the whole series by a semitone, and thus be able to play a good many notes in key B.

The invention of valves for brass instruments has considerably extended the range of usefulness of these instruments. It is now possible for the player to obtain a complete chromatic scale without having to add crooks. The improvement consists in the addition of three (sometimes four) extra pieces of tubing to the instrument; one is of such a length that when added to the whole tube it depresses the entire series by a tone, the second depresses it by a semitone, and the third by three semitones. These additions can be used singly or in any combination, and are brought into action when the player presses down with his finger one or more little pistons communicating with the valves. Take the case of a brass instrument whose fundamental is C (second space, bass stave). The note C (third space, treble stave) is possible because it is the third harmonic, but between this and the next harmonic below (G) there is a gap. But on valve-instruments this can be easily filled in. The player simply blows all the time as for the third harmonic and opens the valves as shown below:

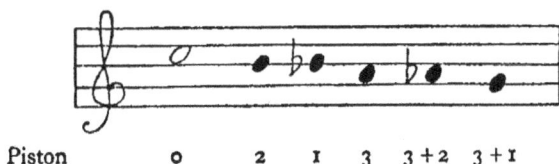

Piston   o   2   1   3   3+2   3+1

(The G can, of course, also be played as a harmonic.)

If a cornet player wished to play the first line of "O God our help," he would blow for the notes shown below—all being harmonics; but by depressing the pistons as numbered, the familiar form of the melody would be obtained:

Pistons used: o   3   3   o   o   o   2   o

Trumpets, French horns, tubas, comets, saxhorns, euphoniums and bombardons and a few other instruments are constructed on the principle explained above.

In the case of trombones, a different plan is generally adopted. The straight part of the tube is double, and by sliding one section of the tube over the other like a telescope the speaking length of the tube can be varied at will. Harmonics are made use of, as in the case of the other brass instruments.

The net result of these improvements in brass instruments has been that such instruments can now be used to play real melodies, not merely fragmentary phrases from the harmonic series, as in Haydn's time. It has also made possible the establishment of satisfactory "Military" and "Brass" bands.

The principles governing the production of notes in the wood-wind instruments can well be studied from a common flageolet or tin-whistle. Holes are bored at definite intervals in the side of the tube. By blowing very gently and covering all the holes the fundamental is obtained. Still blowing as before, one uncovers the hole farthest from the mouthpiece. This has the effect of

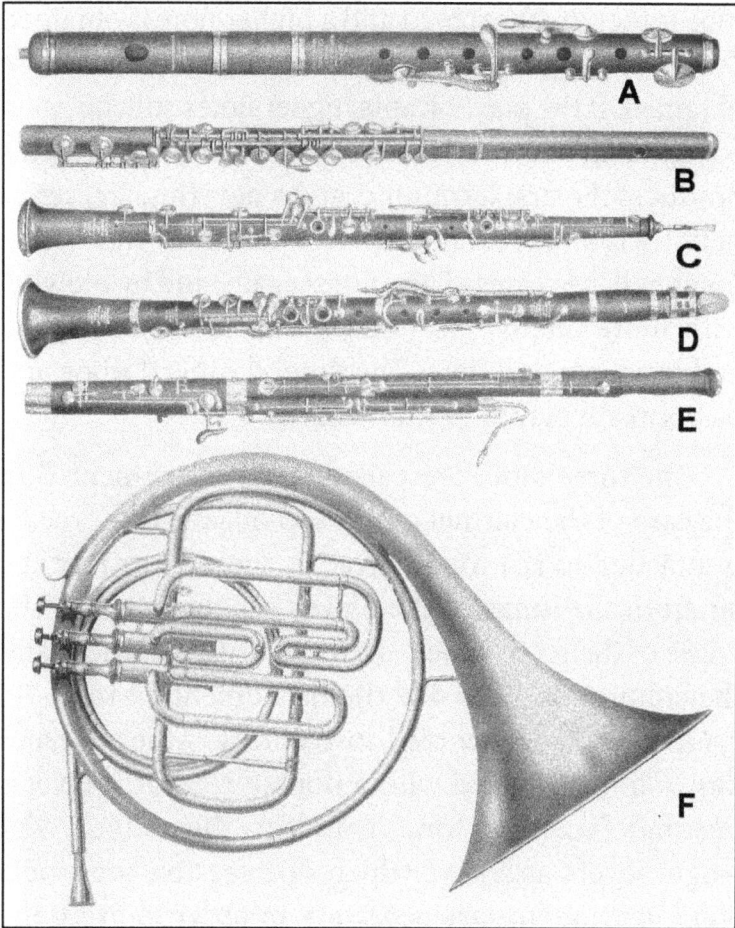

(A) Piccolo. (B) Flute. (c) Oboe. (D) Clarinet.
(E) Bassoon. (F) French Horn.

MODERN WIND INSTRUMENTS

throwing out of action all that part of the tube between the hole and the open end: the speaking length of the tube is thereby shortened and a higher note is obtained. By uncovering the holes in succession, a scale can be obtained. If the player wants higher notes still, he again covers all the holes but blows with more intensity. This produces the first harmonic, and a new (higher) series of notes is obtained. If the player desires to play higher notes still, he closes all the holes again, and by blowing with more intensity produces the second harmonic, and proceeds as before. The flute, clarinet,[76] oboe and bassoon are played in this fashion.

The three latter are called "reed-instruments." In the case of the clarinet a thin slip of cane (the "reed") is attached to the mouthpiece in such a way that the air from the lungs of the player has to pass over the edges of the reed, which is thus set into vibration, and the column of air inside the instrument vibrates "in sympathy." The other reed-instruments—the oboe and bassoon—are played with a double-reed; this gives a peculiar "wheezy" tone-quality to the sounds. The bright levers and keys which one sees on the wood-wind instruments are necessary in order to bring the holes within reach of the player's fingers.

It is unnecessary to describe the method of tone-production in the instruments of percussion. The hemispherical drums (tympani), of which at least two

---

[76] The bore of the clarinet is of such a shape that the even-numbered harmonics only are obtainable. This means that the gap between the harmonics is wider, and more holes in the tube are necessary.

are to be found in the modern orchestra, can be tuned to give notes of definite pitch. The tuning is performed by means of screws which tighten or loosen the parchment forming the surface of the drum.

With regard to the pitch of the wood-wind instruments, roughly speaking, the flute and oboe are treble instruments, the clarinet has a big compass covering nearly all the notes sung by tenor, alto and treble voices, while the bassoon corresponds in pitch to the notes sung by tenors and basses.

A modern orchestra with a full complement of players will comprise:

Two flutes and perhaps a piccolo;

Two oboes and perhaps an alto oboe (cor anglais);

Two clarinets and perhaps a bass clarinet;

Two bassoons, and perhaps a double-bassoon;

Four French horns;

Two trumpets;

Three trombones, and possibly a bass tuba;

A large number of violins;

A smaller number of violas, violoncellos and double-basses;

Two tympani at least;

One or two harps (perhaps);

Various instruments of percussion, e.g. triangle, cymbals, etc.

The "Military Band" consists entirely of wood-wind and brass instruments, with several instruments of percussion. Generally speaking, the clarinets, of which a large number are included, play the passages which in an orchestra would be allotted to the violins. In some military bands, one or two double-basses are included in order to strengthen the bass part.

The "Brass Band" is constituted almost entirely of instruments of the cornet type, made in different sizes in order to cover a wide range of pitch. One or two trumpets and three trombones are usually included, and the percussion department is strongly represented.

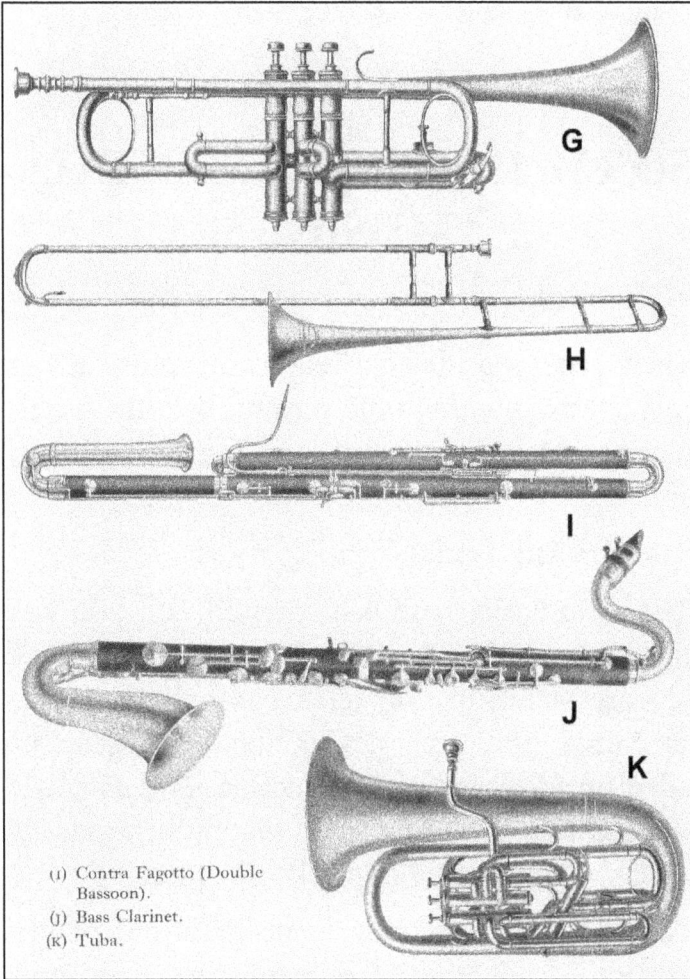

(I) Contra Fagotto (Double
Bassoon).
(J) Bass Clarinet.
(K) Tuba.

(G) TRUMPET.   (H)   TROMBONE.
(I) CONTRA FAGOTTO (DOUBLE BASSOON).
(J) BASS CLARINET.   (K) TUBA.

MODERN WIND INSTRUMENTS

APPENDIX II

FORM IN INSTRUMENTAL MUSIC

I. UNARY FORM.

The piece is founded entirely on one musical idea; the characteristics—rhythmic, melodic or both—persist throughout. Many short Studies and Preludes furnish examples.

II. OLD BINARY FORM.

The essential feature is a division into two well-defined sections. The formula is $A + B$: $\|$: $X + b$. B and X are usually in a key related to the principal key. X may consist of entirely new matter, but is generally founded on ideas in the first section. b is usually B transposed into the tonic key. Frequently, especially with Bach, A and B are not markedly different.

Nearly all the dance movements in the older Suites, e.g. Bach's *French Suites,* are in this form; also most four-line hymn-tunes and Country Dances.

III. TERNARY FORM.

The formula is $A + B + A$; there are three sections, the first and last more or less alike, e.g. "Minuet and Trio." Many Marches, e.g. Chopin's *Marche Funèbre,* the slow movements of many Sonatas, also pieces of the type of *Songs without Words* are in Ternary Form.

IV. AIR WITH VARIATIONS.

This form has been used frequently since early times. Commonly met with in Harpsichord music; also in movements of Sonatas and Symphonies, e.g. in the Finale of Beethoven's 3rd Symphony. Often used as an independent form, e.g. Brahms' *Variations on a Chorale,* Elgar's Enigma Variations.[77]

V. RONDO FORM.

The formula is $A + B + A + C + A + D$ .... The chief feature is the frequent repetition of the first tune, with subsidiary tunes between the repetitions. *B, C, D,* etc. are often developed from *A.*

This form is not often used in modern music. The last movement of the older classical Sonatas and Symphonies is frequently a Rondo, e.g. the last movement of Beethoven's *Sonata Pathétique.*

VI. FUGUE.

A "subject" is given out in one "voice"; this is taken up by each of the "voices" in turn, while those that have had the subject continue with subsidiary matter in contrapuntal fashion. "Episodes" then occur in which the themes are handled in various keys, and the subsidiary themes are freely treated. The essential feature is continuity; strong contrasts are seldom introduced, while the treatment is contrapuntal throughout.

Examples: Bach's *Forty-Eight Preludes and Fugues;* César Franck's *Prelude, Choral and Fugue.*

---

[77] Record H.M.V. Nos. D 578, 582, 602, 596.

VII. Modern Binary Form.

The formula is $A + B \parallel$ development $\parallel A + b$. This differs from the Old Binary form in having a middle section in which themes A and B are transformed and developed. The first section often contains more than two important themes. These additional themes are in a key different from the original, but reappear in the third section in the tonic key.

This form is usually adopted for long instrumental works, especially for Sonatas and Symphonies. It is capable of many modifications. The characteristic feature is, however, (1) a statement of the main themes; (2) development of these; (3) a recapitulation (frequently curtailed) of the subject-matter of the first section. Classical Sonatas and Symphonies have at least one of their movements in Modern Binary Form, strict or free.

VIII. Sonata Form.

A Sonata is a lengthy work for not more than two instruments, comprising two, three or four contrasted movements. These movements may be based on any recognised form, but Modern Binary Form is much used.

Most of the classical "Chamber Music" is written in Sonata Form (in earlier times the term "Sonata" was used very loosely). Beethoven's *Sonata Pathétique* is a good example of this form. As in this case, a slow Introduction is frequently added.

IX. Symphony Form.

A Symphony may be described as a work in Sonata Form for full orchestra.

The term "development" in connection with musical Form is so often used that it may be well to indicate how Schubert develops the first theme of his *Unfinished Symphony*. The theme is:

The successive developments are:

* The accompanying parts are omitted.

Eight bars later, the rhythm only is preserved, thus:

The above is twice repeated on a different chordal basis. Afterwards the original theme is played by the basses; the violins have an accompaniment in semi-quavers. Then:

* The rhythmic figure 𝅘𝅥𝅭 𝅘𝅥 is prominent here.

X. CONCERTO.

Practically a Sonata for one (usually) or more instruments accompanied by an orchestra.

E.g. Bach's *Brandenburg Concertos* (for groups of solo instruments with orchestral accompaniment); Violin Concertos by Beethoven, Mendelssohn, Brahms, and Elgar; Pianoforte Concertos by Mozart and Beethoven, etc. The older Concertos have most of their movements in the Old Binary Form: modern Concertos generally adhere to Sonata Form.

XI. SUITE.

The older Suites (e.g. Bach's) consisted of a group of contrasted pieces founded on dance-forms. The term is now applied to any work consisting of a set of pieces with some common idea underlying them all, e.g. German's *Henry VIII Dances*, Tschaikowsky's *Nut-Cracker Suite (Casse Noisette)*, Holst's *Planets*, etc.

XII. OVERTURE.

Originally this term was applied to the instrumental movement which *opened* an Opera or Oratorio. It is now extended to cover any instrumental piece of some length in one movement, whether connected with an Opera or not. A Concert-Overture is usually written in Modern Binary Form, possibly modified.

The Introduction to Handel's *Messiah* is a good specimen of the older form of Overture; Mendelssohn's *Hebrides*, and Elgar's *Cockaigne* illustrate the Concert-Overture.

XIII. SYMPHONIC POEM or TONE-POEM.

See pp. 146-148.

XIV. MIXED FORMS.

Many works, especially short pieces or movements of moderate length, are to be found in which the form is very elastic and vague. So-called "Impressionist music" belongs to this type; also many pieces termed "Preludes" or "Fantasias" or "Intermezzi." The listener should not over-estimate the value of the practice, now almost universal, of giving a "fancy" title to an instrumental piece. The addition of a title does not necessarily mean that the composer intended to write "programme music"; in fact, he frequently adds the title *afterwards,* on the principle that everything ought to have a name. The title may or may not give a clue to the prevailing mood of the piece; it may or may not suggest that the writer had in his mind a story or train of ideas taking the form of a visual image. Pianoforte "Ballades" have little to do with Song; neither do most "Nocturnes" have any obvious connection with "Night." One is led to make this somewhat trite remark, because some keen listeners who cannot square their impressions with the title given are apt to assume, quite unnecessarily, that their musical sensibility is weak.

GRAMOPHONE RECORDS

THE Gramophone, as well as the Player-Piano, is of inestimable value when rightly used. These instruments have revolutionised the study of Musical History; instead of *reading about* musical works, one can *hear* them. But even in the case of the best records, one must regard them merely as a substitute for the real thing. There is a want of balance between the parts; the brass instruments in particular do not record well, neither do any of the bass instruments. The tone-colour of every instrument except, perhaps, the clarinet, possibly the flute also, is not exactly preserved, although great improvements have lately been made in this direction.

The chief virtue of the Gramophone is that it enables us to study a work before listening to an actual performance; thus we can conveniently—and cheaply—acquire that degree of familiarity with the music without which it cannot be fully comprehended. Especially is this the case with complicated modern music. In studying a work by means of the Gramophone, it is advisable to follow the music whenever possible from a printed copy; in the case of an orchestral work preferably from a miniature full-score. In that way, a good deal of knowledge of the fascinating art of Instrumentation can be learnt. If any particular section of a work seems at first less attractive than other sections, it should be played again several times until it becomes familiar. Probably, many vital details were not grasped at the first hearing. Records 26, 29, 33, 34, and many others particularly demand this treatment.

Judgment should be exercised in the choice of needles. In a small room a "medium needle" will give quite enough volume of tone, and often even a softer needle will improve the balance. In order to camouflage the want of power in the case of low notes it is well to reinforce these, sometimes, by playing them on the pianoforte. Most records of long works are severely "cut"; this, besides giving a wrong idea of the relative proportion between the different sections, means that a careful comparison between the record and the printed copy must be made in order to avoid "losing the place." Nevertheless, an increasing number of records of complete works is being issued.

Difficulty is often found in hearing the words clearly when a vocal record is in question. Of course, this is only to be expected in the case of words in an unfamiliar language, but the makers of records now frequently issue explanatory notes. These should always be asked for when a new record is bought. E.g. it is quite easy to follow the latest Wagnerian records from the descriptive pamphlets. Hitherto it has been found almost impossible to get a clear reproduction of the sibilant sounds, *s, z, sh*. If one is always on the alert to supply these sounds mentally it is remarkable how much easier it becomes to distinguish English words.

The following list of records has been compiled mainly from the point of view of the history of musical development; therefore many popular works of no peculiar significance have not been included. What has been attempted is to supply a *representative* list. Probably a limited selection will have to be made; those records marked ** should certainly be obtained, followed by those marked *. Many of the records listed in catalogues were made before the art of reproduction was well understood; the moral is that where there is a choice, the purchaser should obtain the *latest* record of any work. There is no need to make a fetish of buying expensive "Celebrity" records; some "celebrities" do not "record" so well as their more modest colleagues.

All the records are "His Master's Voice" except those marked Voc. which are "Vocalion," those marked Col., i.e. "Columbia," and the "Brunswick" records.

MASSES

1	**"Aeterna Christi"	Palestrina	D 338	
2	Mass in 4 parts	Byrd	E 296 (*Agnus Dei*)	

MOTETS

3	*"Exsurge Domine" ...	Byrd	D 710
4	"Turn our captivity" (and two Madrigals)	,,	D 711

MADRIGALS

5	"In going to my lonely bed"	Edwards	E 267
6	"On the plains"	Weelkes	E 233
7	**"Tho' Amaryllis dance" } "This merry month" }	Byrd	E 292

These three discs comprise six Madrigals.

HARPSICHORD MUSIC

8	Sonata in D major ...	Scarlatti }	E 204
9	Sonata in A major ...		
10	*Fugues in D and E minor...	Bach	D 491
11	**English Folk Dances ...	—	E 208

EARLY CHAMBER MUSIC

12	Fantasia for String Sextet	Byrd	E 293

EARLY CLASSICAL MUSIC (STRINGS)

13	Andantino } (for Violin) ...	Martini }	2955 (Col.)
	Minuetto }	Pugnani }	
14	Aria on G string (Violin) ...	Bach	3149 (Col.)
15	**Concerto for 2 Violins ...	,,	DB 587, 588
16	Violin Sonata, D major ...	Handel	E 279, 280
17	Gigue in C major ('Cello)...	Bach	D 346

CLASSICAL CHAMBER MUSIC

18	Rondo (Violin)	Mozart	D 02047 (Voc.)
19	**"Emperor" Quartet ...	Haydn	DB 651 (*Slow movement*)
20	*Quartet in D (No. 15) ...	Mozart	L 1330, 1331 (Col.)
21	Quartet in D	Beethoven	D 02008 (Voc.) (*Allegro and Presto only*)
22	**Kreutzer Sonata	,,	L 1210, 1211 (Col.)
23	Quartet in A major ...	Schumann	D 13
24	Trio (Violin, 'Cello, Piano)	Mendelssohn	D 02008, 02054 (Voc.)
25	*Quartet in D minor ...	Schubert	D 88 (*Variations only*)

MODERN CHAMBER MUSIC

26	**Clarinet and Strings (Quintet)	Brahms	L 1219 (Col.)
27	Quartet (Strings)	Dvořák	L 1465 (Col.) (*Lento only*)
28	** { Andante Cantabile ...	Tschaikowsky }	L 1004 (Col.)
	{ Andante	Debussy }	
29	*Sonata in A major	César Franck	C 895, 896
30	"Orientale" from }	Glazounoff	E 199
31	String Quartet }		
32	Violin Sonata in F	Grieg	L 1440 (Col.)
33	**Quartet in E minor ...	Elgar	D 02027 (Voc.) (*2nd and 3rd movements*)
34	*Violin Sonata, No. 2 ...	Ireland	L 1322, 1323 (Col.)

CONCERTOS

35	Brandenburg Concerto	Bach	D 683, 684
36	*Violin Concerto	Beethoven	D 767 to 771
37	**Violin Concerto	Elgar	1071, 1072 (Col.)

SYMPHONIES

38	"Eroica" Symphony ...	Beethoven	(Recorded complete by Col.)
39	**Fifth Symphony	,,	D 665 to 668
40	**"Unfinished"	Schubert	J 04037, 04038 (Voc.)
41	Symphonie Pathétique ...	Tschaikowsky	D 713 to 716
42	*"New World" Symphony	Dvořák	(Recorded complete by Col.)

OVERTURES

43	"Figaro"	Mozart	J 04021 (Voc.)
44	**"Coriolan"	Beethoven	L 1021 (Col.)
45	"Rosamunde"	Schubert	273 (Col.)
46	*"Der Freischütz"	Weber	424 (Col.)
47	"Lohengrin"	Wagner	D 129
48	**"Die Meistersinger" ...	,,	D 590
49	**"Cockaigne"	Elgar	D 493
50	"Pierrot of the Minute" ...	Bantock	L 1463 (Col.)

SUITES

51	"L'Arlésienne"	Bizet	D 147, 148
52	"Casse Noisette"	Tschaikowsky	D 125, 126, 127
53	**"Scheherazade"	Rimsky-Korsakoff	D 131, 132
54	Gipsy Suite	E. German	D 473, 492
55	*"Peer Gynt"	Grieg	D 156, 157
56	Petite Suite	Debussy	J 04011
57	*"Mother Goose"	Ravel	D 708, 709
58	"The Planets"	Holst	(Recorded in separate numbers) (Col.)
59	**"The Fire Bird"	Stravinski	L 1040 (Col.)
60	"Conversations"	Bliss	L 1475, 1476 (Col.)

MISCELLANEOUS

61	**"L'Après-midi d'une faune"	Debussy	D 130
62	Venusberg Music	Wagner	L 1378 (Col.)
63	"A Shropshire Lad" ...	Butterworth	D 520
64	**"Siegfried Idyll"	Wagner	L 1425, 1426 (Col.)

SYMPHONIC POEMS

65	"Le Chasseur maudit" ...	César Franck	L 1423 (Col.)
66	"Finlandia"	Sibelius	D 142
67	*"Tod und Verklärung" ...	Strauss	D 743, 744
68	**"Till Eulenspiegel" ...	,,	D 608, 609
69	*"L'Apprenti Sorcier" ...	Dukas	D 461
70	**"Poème de l'Extase" ...	Scriabin	L 1380, 1381 (Col.)

217

OPERAS

Aïda, Carmen and *Rigoletto* and some of the Gilbert and Sullivan Operas have been recorded in full by Col., and *Carmen, Cavalleria, Faust* (Gounod), *Il Trovatore* and *Pagliacci* by H.M.V.; but, if expense is an object, the money would be better expended in procuring some of the extracts from typical Operas named below. Nos. 71 to 81, also 87 to 90, are Arias; Nos. 82 to 86 are concerted items.

71	**"Non mi dir" ... ... (*Don Giovanni*)	Mozart	7230 (Col.)
72	*"Che faro" (*Euridice*) ...	Gluck	7217 (Col.)
73	"Nature immense" ... ... (*Faust*)	Berlioz	DB 487
74	**"Celeste Aïda" ... ... (*Aïda*)	Verdi	A/0111 (Voc.)
75	"Caro Nonne" ... ... (*Rigoletto*)	„	C/01044 (Voc.)
76	**"O luce" (*Linda*) ...	Donizetti	DB 597
77	"Bénédiction des poignards" (*Les Huguenots*)	Meyerbeer	2/032009
78	**"Willow Song" ... ... (*Otello*)	Verdi	C 01083
79	"Dance of the Seven Veils"... (*Salome*)	R. Strauss	Col./1422
80	*"When the stars" ... ... (*Tosca*)	Puccini	D 707
81	"Der kleine Sandmann" ... (*Hänsel und Gretel*)	Humperdinck	DB 756
82	"Questa è una ragna" (Trio) (*Otello*)	Verdi	DA 412
83	**"Bella figlia" (Quartet) ... (*Rigoletto*)	„	DM 118
84	"Nume Custodi" (Trio and Chorus) (*Aïda*)	„	D 5562 (Col.)
85	"No davver" (Duet and Chorus) (*Carmen*)	Bizet	D 5597 (Col.)
86	*Quintet from *Meistersinger* ...	Wagner	D 756
87	**"Death of Boris" ... ... (*Boris Goudonof*)	Moussorgsky	DB 100
88	"In the town of Kazan" ... (*Boris Goudonof*)	„	7/22009
89	"Song of Vladimir" ... ... (*Prince Igor*)	Borodin	022208
90	*"Chanson indoue" ... ... (*Sadko*)	Rimsky-Korsakoff	DA 233

WAGNERIAN RECORDS

The following will give a good insight into Wagner's methods:

91	**Overture "Tannhäuser"	...		296 (Col.)
92	Overture "Lohengrin"	...		453 (Col.)
93	Lohengrin's Farewell...	...		L 1147 (Col.)
94	*Venusberg Music	...	from *Tannhäuser*	L 1378 (Col.)
95	**Love Duet—Act II ...	...	from *Tristan*	D 736, 737
96	Overture	... ...	from *Meistersinger*	D 139
97	**Prize Song	...	,,	D 758
98	"Am stillen Herd" ...	...		D 747
99	Entry of the Gods ...	...	from *Das Rheingold*	D 503
100	Wotan's Farewell	...	from *Die Walküre*	4/42529
101	Ride of the Valkyries...	...	,,	D 681
102	**Fire-Music	..	,,	DB 439
103	*Siegmund greets the Spring...		,,	D 679
104	Siegfried and the Birds	...	from *Siegfried*	D 701
105	**Siegfried forges the sword	...	,,	D 700
106	**Siegfried Idyll	... ...	(A "Serenade")	1425, 1426 (Col.)

CHORAL MUSIC

Very little of choral music of importance has been recorded. Good examples of the old-fashioned Oratorio Aria are:

"With Verdure clad" (Haydn's *Creation*). C 01072 (Voc.).

"Why do the Nations" (Handel's *Messiah*). D 02087 (Voc.).

Many excerpts from *Messiah* and Mendelssohn's *Elijah* have been recorded by H.M.V. Modern Oratorio is represented by "Kyrie" from Elgar's *Dream of Gerontius* (C 977).

PIANOFORTE

Unfortunately, the pianoforte does not "record" well; the player-piano is, of course, far preferable here. However, the *very latest* gramophone records exhibit great improvements. It would seem impossible to obtain a record from the Clavichord; its tone is much too thin, but the Harpsichord records are fairly faithful to the original.

107	**"Moonlight" Sonata... ...	Beethoven	D/66
108	†Three Études } Nocturne and Polonaise } ...	Chopin	D/82
109	{"La Campanella"	Liszt	D/65
	{"Carnavai" (Finale) ...	Schumann	D/49
110	**Capriccio	Brahms	L/1124 (Col.)
111	*{Prelude in G minor ...	Rachmaninoff }	L/1220 (Col.)
	{"La Cathédrale engloutie"	Debussy }	
112	"Minstrels"	„	E/216
113	**"Jeux d'eau"	Ravel	DB 643
114	Fantasia Baetica	Falla	D/766

SONGS

In spite of the fact that the bulk of music "recorded" consists of Songs and Arias, it is impossible to compile a satisfactory list of records which will illustrate the growth of the artistic song. Most of the thousands of song-records issued are of the "drawing-room ballad" type, and are quite outside the sphere of art in which moved such great writers of song as Schubert, Schumann, Brahms and Wolf.

115	**"Bingo" } "Admiral Benbow" } ...	English Folk Songs	R/6012 (Voc.)
116	*"Lord Rendal"	A Folk Ballad	A/0167 (Voc.)
117	"Go down, Moses" ...	A Negro Spirituel	B/3032 (Voc.)
118	"Arise!"	Purcell	L/1414 (Col.)
119	"Tom Bowling"	Dibdin	E/60
120	"Believe me"...	Moore	R/6082 (Voc.)
121	**"Lass with the delicate air"...	Arne	R/6015 (Voc.)
122	**"Erl-King"	Schubert	D/257
123	"Serenade"	„	DA 458
124	*"Two Grenadiers"	Schumann	K/05023 (Voc.)
125	**{"Lo here the gentle lark"	Bishop	130 (Col.)
	{"Sweet bird"	Handel }	
126	"A Memory"	Goring Thomas	E 314
127	*"By the waters of Babylon"	Dvořák	D/104
128	**"Sea Pictures"	Elgar	D/02052 (Voc.)
129	"All Souls' Day"	Strauss	E 51
130	"On Wenlock Edge"† ...	Vaughan-Williams	7146, 7147, 7148, 7149, 7150 (Col.)
131	"Now sleeps the crimson petal"	Quilter	DA 434
132	*"Love went a-riding" ...	Frank Bridge	L/1325 (Col.)
133	**"Song of a poor wanderer"‡	Nevstruev	A/0133 (Voc.)
134	"The Goat"§...	Moussorgsky	A/0140 (Voc.)
135	"Der Nussbaum"	Schumann	C/01092 (Voc.)
136	"Der Tod und das Mädchen"	Schubert	L/5036 (Voc.)

Obviously, many of the most important works are too lengthy for reproduction on the Gramophone. This is especially the case with long choral works. However, these are obtainable in the form of "Vocal Scores" in several editions. No one with any pretensions to musical culture can afford to be ignorant of the following masterpieces:

Bach	"Matthew Passion."
,, ...	Mass in B minor*.
,, ...	"Sing to the Lord" (Motet).
Handel	"Messiah" and "Israel in Egypt."
Haydn	"Creation."
Mozart	"Requiem."
Beethoven	Mass in D.
,, ...	Choral Symphony.
Mendelssohn... ...	"Elijah."
,, ...	"Hymn of Praise."
Brahms	"Requiem."
Dvořák	"Stabat Mater."
Parry	"Job."
Elgar	"Dream of Gerontius."
Holst	"Hymn of Jesus" (Stainer and Bell).
Vaughan-Williams ...	Mass in G minor (Curwen).

Supplementary List of Records

The following list includes many of the best records lately issued. All can be recommended. In nearly all cases the records are "double-sided."

(1) Symphony No. 5 in E minor (Tschaikowsky). [This has been recorded complete on six double-sided discs: D 759 to 764.]

(2) French and Scottish Dances (McEwen) for String Quartet. R 6140.

(3) Larghetto for two violins and pianoforte (Spohr). D 02144.

221

(4) Trio (part of) by Mozart, for Violin, Viola and Pianoforte. D 02150.

(5) String Quartet in D major (Tschaikowsky). [This is recorded without "cuts" on records Nos. D 865-868.]

(6) "Sapphische Ode" (Brahms) and "All Souls' Day" (Lassen). [These songs are recorded on record DA 597.]

(7) Prelude and Fugue in B flat major, also a Fantasia, by Bach, played by Harold Samuel. D 863.

(8) Folk-Song Suite for Military Band, by Vaughan-Williams. Col. K 05086. [A fine record, not at all blatant.]

(9) "Le Rossignol" (Liszt). R 6106 Voc. [A good Pianoforte record.]

(10) String Quartet in D major, by Haydn. [This is recorded complete by Col. L 1559-1561.]

(11) "Is not His word like a fire?" (from Mendelssohn's *Elijah*). R 6145.

(12) "Le Bourgeois Gentilhomme." [A set of piquant movements for Orchestra by Richard Strauss.] Col. L 1152-1155.

(13) Beethoven's Eighth Symphony, recorded complete by Col. L 1538-1541.

(14) "Egmont" Overture, by Beethoven. D 852.

(15) Two Arias by Bellini and Verdi respectively, sung by Galli-Curci. [Very fine.] DB 557.

(16) "Du meine Seele" (Schumann).
"Schlafe, mein Prinzchen" (Mozart).
[Good examples of the classical song. DA 557.]

(17) Suite in B minor for Flute and Strings, by Bach. L 1557, 1558.

(18) Beethoven's Seventh Symphony is recorded without "cuts" by Col.

(19) Beethoven's Choral Symphony is recorded complete by H.M.V.

(20) "Carnaval" (Schumann), played by Cortot. DB 706.

(21) Hungarian Rhapsody No. 1 (Liszt). 50023 B–Brunswick. [Records Nos. 20 and 21 show that the recording of Pianoforte music has been much improved lately.]

(22) "Slumber Song" (Schumann). R 646 Voc. [This well exhibits the tone-colour of the Viola.]

(23) Choruses from Handel's Messiah: "His yoke is easy," "Surely He hath borne our griefs," "Lift up your heads" and "All we like sheep." DB 779 and 780.

(24) The Russian Ballet music "Petrouchka," by Stravinski, has been well recorded by H.M.V.

(25) "Le Coq d'or," by Rimsky-Korsakoff. D 732.

(26) Finale of Brahms' Symphony No. 2. D 874.

(27) Handel's "Water Music." L 1437, 1438 Col.

(28) Variations Symphoniques, by César Franck. D 697, 698.

(29) Lento and Scherzo movements of Dvořák's Quartet in F. Brunswick 25015 *a*.

(30) "La Gitana" (Kreisler)
    "Souvenir" (Drdla)
        Violin solos. Brunswick 15003.

(30*a*) "Canzonetta" from Tschaikowsky's Violin Concerto. Brunswick 50026.

(31) "Ingemisco" (bass solo from Verdi's *Requiem*). Brunswick 35002 B.

(32) Two Bourrés and the Fugue from the Chromatic Fantasia by Bach, played by Harold Samuel. D 783.

(33) Trio No. 7 by Mozart. D 02150 (Vocalion).

(34) "Why do the nations" (Messiah). D 02087 (Vocalion).

(35) "Edward"—dramatic Ballad by Löwe. L 1466 Col.

(36) Brahms' Second Symphony (complete). D 871-2-3-4.

(37) Mozart's Symphony in E flat. No. 39 (complete). L 1563-4-5 Col.

(38) "L'oiseau de Feu," by Stravinski. L 1040 Col.

(39) The following are fine examples of the successful recording of music for Strings:

   (*a*) "Mazurka" by Chopin and "Melodie" by Paderewski, arranged for Violin. DA 511.

(*b*) "Sérénade Espagnole" (Glazounoff) and "Gavotte" (Henschel) for 'Cello. DA 570.

(*c*) "Hebrew Melody" and "Grand Adagio" (Glazounoff) for Violin. DA 596.

(*d*) "Romance" (Svendsen) and "Mazurka" for Violin. D 712.

APPENDIX IV

THE LISTENER

MUSICAL interest is stimulated either emotionally or intellectually, sometimes in both ways. A listener who has no knowledge of musical technique, no acquaintance with Form or with musical history, and no familiarity with the scientific aspect of music may yet have his emotions profoundly stirred when listening to fine works. On the other hand, it is possible to derive much intellectual pleasure from a knowledge of the technical side of the art. Some music, e.g. much of Bach's *Matthew Passion,* is so strong in its emotional appeal that its intellectual features are hardly noticed until one looks for them. But there is a good deal of fine music in which the appeal to the intellect is stronger than the appeal to the emotions. Bach's *Art of Fugue* is an extreme instance of this; the interest is mainly centred in the solution of difficult musical problems.

These two aspects of music—the emotional and the intellectual—do not exclude each other. A really cultured listener experiences both forms of pleasure, although it will often happen that at any particular moment one or the other will predominate. An elaborate

Fugue will, as a rule, make little appeal to the listener who can respond only to an emotional stimulus, but its intellectual qualities may be intensely interesting to one whose training enables him to detect these.

No composer can be all the time in a state of high emotional excitement; this would be unnatural and exhausting. He must relax sometimes, and it is at such moments that he often allows intellectual interest to predominate to the confusion of the superficial listener. This frequently happens in the "working-out" section of a Sonata or Symphony, and also in some modern works where the contrapuntal principle is freely adopted. In order that the listener should be able in such cases to follow the composer's line of thought; to enter, as it were, into the composer's mind and discover his method of working, it is necessary that he should have some knowledge of the principles underlying musical development, the transformation and combination of themes, tonality, tone-colour, and so forth.

It cannot be too strongly emphasised that some degree of familiarity is essential to the full appreciation of any work of art. Psychologists assert that the feeling of satisfaction with which one recognises a familiar object can be one of the strongest of pleasurable emotions. On the other hand, an object entirely devoid of any familiar feature interests us not at all. It is somewhat remarkable, and is certainly fortunate, that in the case of Music the necessary degree of familiarity can be quickly attained. A very few repetitions of a harmonic progression which at first sounds intolerably ugly will make it quite bearable. Bewilderment is one of the least pleasurable emotions, therefore we must try to conquer this by familiarity; that is, we must hear a complicated passage over and over again before we can hope to get any enjoyment from it. Many composers assume that listeners have the ability to remember the chief themes upon which the music is built after hearing them announced once only; and moreover, some of their themes are cast in an unfamiliar mould and are presented with other subordinate themes which at first distract the attention. Little pleasure will be obtained from hearing a long orchestral work unless the main themes are learnt by heart so that they can be recognised in whatever guise they appear. As soon as these themes have become thoroughly familiar, do not pay too much attention to them when they occur (they will stand out of themselves), but listen particularly to the subordinate themes which accompany them.

It often happens that one is not able to study before-hand a work which one is going to hear for the first time. In that case be prepared to listen with an open mind; do not judge of the value of a work by comparing it with another planned on a different scale and written in another idiom. E.g. one will get little pleasure from hearing Vaughan-Williams' *Mass in G minor* if one is consciously or unconsciously comparing it all the time with Bach's *B minor Mass*. One may safely compare *The Mikado* with *Patience* but not with *Die Meistersinger.*

Do not judge of orchestral works from an arrange-ment for Piano Solo; a Gramophone record is much better, especially if one can follow the music from a miniature full-score. In reading from a miniature score, observe that the parts for wood-wind are to be found at the top of the page; immediately below come those for the brass, then come the parts for percussion instruments. The string parts occupy the lowest staves on the page. The best method of following the score is to fix the attention normally on the first violin part, which more often than not contains the chief tunes. It will easily be seen by the look of the score whether the violins are merely playing an accompaniment. In that case the interest will often lie in the wood-wind parts if the other instruments are "resting" or playing quietly. But the 'cellos and French horns sometimes have the principal melody. If you detect the mark f or ff in the middle section of the score (devoted to the brass) and the part looks melodic, you may suspect that here is an important theme. If the full orchestra is engaged, it is quite unlikely that the wood-wind will be prominently heard; these instruments will probably only be "doubling" some other parts. In fact, phrases played by the wood-wind only "tell" when very lightly accompanied. A phrase played by the flute, 'cello, or French horn in the highest register is nearly always important. As a rule, the prominence of a melody depends not so much on the particular instrument employed as upon the doings of the other instruments. A tune played softly on the oboe or bassoon is quite telling if very delicately accompanied. Notice that a passage played by all the strings in unison or octaves always stands out. A full score by Haydn, Mozart or Beethoven is comparatively easy to follow, especial if one has played the work previously on the pianoforte.

A fascinating and valuable method of studying a full score is to read it through at home, underlining lightly with a blue pencil the themes which you think will come into prominence, and then at the actual performance compare the effect you imagined with that really produced.

In the case of Symphonic Poems, try to obtain beforehand a synopsis of the "plot" and endeavour to follow this while an arrangement is played on the Gramophone, Piano-player, or the Pianoforte (a pianoforte-duet arrangement is generally satisfactory). But at the Concert, do *not* consult the analysis. From the point of view of getting to understand the composer's technique, listening to music is of little value unless one follows it from the printed copy. If one listens with a definite object—to acquire, say, the art of reading from score—there can be no doubt of its efficacy.

A great deal of harm is done by people who profess that the little sphere of musical literature in which they are specialists is the only form of art which matters. Strive to cultivate a catholic taste, but hold in healthy abhorrence all music (so-called) which appears to you as "cheap." Also, do not get into the habit of idolising some great performer and pretending that he alone is the worthy exponent of certain musical works. Such notions would soon disappear if performers played or sang behind a screen. Endeavour to attend to the music, not to the performer, and listen frequently with eyes closed. Do not imagine that an extensive acquaintance with the latest productions will give you a right to pose as "advanced." The really advanced listeners are usually devotees of Bach and Mozart. On the other hand, do not pretend to like a work merely because you are told that you ought to, you cannot *reason* yourself into appreciating anything. Neither need you withhold your admiration of an unpretentious work which makes an ever-growing appeal. The very fact that it makes some appeal is a proof that it arouses emotions struggling for expression. Good taste in music needs preservation rather than acquirement. By nature the child usually has good musical taste, but unless this is nourished by the continual hearing of works which conform to a recognised standard of merit, it is bound to degenerate. Toleration of really poor music is the mark of a lazy listener. If one is not prepared to expend as much mental effort on hearing a Symphony as on following a three-act play, then appreciation of the music will diminish accordingly.

Simply because a particular modern work is devoid of any striking melodies, while evincing any amount of harmonic ingenuity, it does not follow that the work is epoch-making. A good tune is the greatest gift which music has to offer, and if not allied to words unworthy of it its influence can never be other than wholesome. This cannot be said of a good deal of the music written by Stravinski and others who imitate him. Here the appeal is too often to the coarser emotions—brutality, horror and thinly-disguised lust. To pose as an out-and-out admirer of this school is to confess to a lack of mental and moral balance.

BIBLIOGRAPHY

ONLY such books are included as would be reasonably intelligible to the layman.

Music and its Appreciation. STEWART MACPHERSON. (*Joseph Williams.*)

Music: what it means. LEIGH HENRY. (*Curwen and Sons.*)

The Books of the Great Musicians. (3 vols.) PERCY SCHOLES. (*Oxford University Press.*)

The Growth of Music. (3 vols.) H. C. COLLES. (*Oxford University Press.*)

Studies of Great Composers. PARRY. (*Routledge.*)

Beethoven and his nine Symphonies. GROVE. (*Novello.*)

Beethoven and his Forerunners. MASON. (*Macmillan.*)

Foundations of Musical Æsthetics. J. B. McEWEN. (*Kegan Paul.*)

The Scope of Music. BUCK. (*Oxford University Press.*)

Chamber Music. DUNHILL. (*Macmillan.*)

Evolution of the Art of Music. PARRY. (*Kegan Paul.*)

BIBLIOGRAPHY

Listener's Guide to Music. SCHOLES. (*Oxford University Press.*)

The Orchestra. NATHAN. (*Kegan Paul.*)

The Threshold of Music. WALLACE. (*Macmillan.*)

Life of Bach. (2 vols.) SCHWEITZER. (*Novello.*)

Form in Music. MACPHERSON. (*Joseph Williams.*)

English Folk-Song. CECIL SHARP. (*Novello.*)

History of Music. STANFORD AND FORSYTH. (*Macmillan.*)

A Musical Pilgrim's Progress. J. D. RORKE. (*Oxford University Press.*)

Style in Musical Art. PARRY. (*Macmillan.*)

Musical Studies. ERNEST NEWMAN. (*John Lane.*)

History of Music in England. WALKER. (*Oxford University Press.*)

Studies in Modern Music. (2 vols.) HADOW. (*Seely.*)

The Promenade Ticket. SIDGWICK. (*Arnold.*)

Introduction to Russian Music. NATHAN. (*Palmer and Hayward.*)

Life of Mozart. EVERYMAN LIBRARY. (*Dent.*)

French Music of To-day. JEAN AUBRY. (*Kegan Paul.*)

Handel. ROMAIN ROLLAND. (*Kegan Paul.*)

Listening to Music by means of the Gramophone. SCHOLES. (*Gramophone Co.*)

History of Pianoforte Music. WESTERBY. (*Kegan Paul.*)

Music and Mind. YORKE TROTTER. (*Methuen.*)

The Musical Pilgrim. Ed. by A. SOMERVELL (a series of monographs).

Musical Criticism. CALVOCORESSI. (*Oxford University Press.*)

Modern Music. MYERS. (*Kegan Paul.*)

Music and the Plain Man. D. G. MASON. (*H. W. Gray Co.*)

Language of Music. FREDERICK NICHOLLS. (*Kegan Paul.*)

Music Lover's Library. (*Kegan Paul.*):

    (1) Short History of Music. A. E. HULL.

    (2) Design in Music. A. E. HULL.

    (3) Music and Religion. LONGFORD.

    (4) The Story of Mediæval Music. TERRY.

    (5) Short History of Harmony. C. MACPHERSON.

    (6) The Philosophy of Modernism. CYRIL SCOTT.

From Grieg to Brahms. D. G. MASON. (*Macmillan.*)

BOOKS FOR REFERENCE.

Dictionary of Music. GROVE.

Oxford History of Music.

Dictionary of Modern Music. (*Dent.*)